TOM CLANCY

A Critical Companion

Helen S. Garson

CRITICAL COMPANIONS TO POPULAR CONTEMPORARY WRITERS
Kathleen Gregory Klein, Series Editor

Greenwood Press
Westport, Connecticut • London

Library of Congress Cataloging-in-Publication Data

Garson, Helen S.
    Tom Clancy : a critical companion / Helen S. Garson.
        p.   cm.—(Critical companions to popular contemporary
    writers, ISSN 1082–4979)
    Includes bibliographical references and index.
    ISBN 0–313–29505–0 (alk. paper)
    1. Clancy, Tom, 1947–   —Criticism and interpretation.
    2. Adventure stories, American—History and criticism.   3. War
    stories, American—History and criticism.   4. Military art and
    science in literature.   5. Technology in literature.   I. Title.
    II. Series.
    PS3553.L245Z68   1996
    813'.54—dc20   95–50454

British Library Cataloguing in Publication Data is available.

Library of Congress Catalog Card Number: 95–50454
ISBN: 0–313–29505–0
ISSN: 1082–4979

First published in 1996

Greenwood Press, 88 Post Road West, Westport, CT 06881
An imprint of Greenwood Publishing Group, Inc.

Printed in the United States of America

∞™

The paper used in this book complies with the
Permanent Paper Standard issued by the National
Information Standards Organization (Z39.48–1984).

P

For
Danny, Dustin, Evvy, Julie, Katie

ADVISORY BOARD

Contents

Series Foreword

The authors who appear in the series Critical Companions to Popular Contemporary Writers are all best-selling writers. They do not have only one successful novel, but a string of them. Fans, critics, and specialist readers eagerly anticipate their next book. For some, high cash advances and breakthrough sales figures are automatic; movie deals often follow. Some writers become household names, recognized by almost everyone.

But novels are read one by one. Each reader chooses to start and, more importantly, to finish a book because of what she or he finds there. The real test of a novel is in the satisfaction its readers experience. This series acknowledges the extraordinary involvement of readers and writers in creating a best-seller.

The authors included in this series were chosen by an Advisory Board composed of high school English teachers and high school and public librarians. They ranked a list of best-selling writers according to their popularity among different groups of readers. Writers in the top-ranked group who had not received book-length, academic literary analysis (or none in at least the past ten years) were chosen for the series. Because of this selection method, Critical Companions to Popular Contemporary Writers meets a need that is not addressed elsewhere.

The volumes in the series are written by scholars with particular expertise in analyzing popular fiction. These specialists add an academic focus to the popular success that the best-selling writers already enjoy.

The series is designed to appeal to a wide range of readers. The general reading public will find explanations for the appeal of these well-known writers. Fans will find biographical and fictional questions answered. Students will find literary analysis, discussions of fictional genres, carefully organized introductions to new ways of reading the novels, and bibliographies for additional research. Students will also be able to apply what they have learned from this book to their readings of future novels by these best-selling writers.

Each volume begins with a biographical chapter drawing on published information, autobiographies or memoirs, prior interviews, and, in some cases, interviews given especially for this series. A chapter on literary history and genres describes how the author's work fits into a larger literary context. The following chapters analyze the writer's most important, most popular, and most recent novels in detail. Each chapter focuses on a single novel. This approach, suggested by the Advisory Board as the most useful to student research, allows for an in-depth analysis of the writer's fiction. Close and careful readings with numerous examples show readers exactly how the novels work. These chapters are organized around three central elements: plot development (how the story line moves forward), character development (what the reader knows about the important figures), and theme (the significant ideas of the novel). Chapters may also include sections on generic conventions (how the novel is similar to or different from others in its same category of science fiction, fantasy, thriller, etc.), narrative point of view (who tells the story and how), symbols and literary language, and historical or social context. Each chapter ends with an "alternative reading" of the novel. The volume concludes with a primary and secondary bibliography, including reviews.

The Alternative Readings are a unique feature of this series. By demonstrating a particular way of reading each novel, they provide a clear example of how a specific perspective can reveal important aspects of the book. In each alternative reading section, one contemporary literary theory—such as feminist criticism, Marxism, new historicism, deconstruction, or Jungian psychological critique—is defined in brief, easily comprehensible language. That definition is then applied to the novel to highlight specific features that might go unnoticed or be understood differently in a more general reading of the novel. Each volume defines two or three specific theories, making them part of the reader's understanding of how diverse meanings may be constructed from a single novel.

Taken collectively, the volumes in the Critical Companions to Popular Contemporary Writers series provide a wide-ranging investigation of the complexities of current best-selling fiction. By treating these novels seriously as both literary works and publishing successes, the series demonstrates the potential of popular literature in contemporary culture.

Kathleen Gregory Klein
Southern Connecticut State University

Acknowledgments

My thanks to the following people: Anne Rubin for television research; Amelia Rutledge for assistance on science fiction; the librarians at George Mason University and the Reston Regional Library; and, above all, to my husband, H. Neil Garson, for help with the technological material.

TOM
CLANCY

1

About Tom Clancy

In what some interviewers refer to as his staccato delivery, Tom Clancy divides the world into "good guys" and "bad guys." "We," that is, the United States and its political friends, at home and abroad, are the "good guys." "They," are all the others, and that group is large. Clancy's novels, essays, speeches, and published conversations provide the details. But the television persona who uses such terms as "good guys"/"bad guys" says them with a smile and a little laugh. The television medium shows a much more relaxed Clancy than the one on the printed page. Although the words may be the same, the music is different.

Whether we agree or disagree with Clancy's philosophy, we respond to the man up on the screen, bantering with the program host, most often the memorable and adroit Larry King. True, Clancy is generally flacking a current book, even though he points out that his host hasn't read it. (King defends himself, saying he reads the books "later.") King, unlike the fast-moving hosts of daytime television, gives Clancy time for more than a sound bite, and at the end when King signs off, saying, "Tom Clancy—good guy," the viewer probably agrees.

Yet this is an author who arouses strong feelings, positive and negative, in book and film reviewers, critics, reporters, military personnel, government workers, presidents, vice-presidents, congressmen and women, and senators. His loyal followers are so committed that a number of them wrote protest letters to the *Washington Post* after the publication of an unflattering—though humorous—interview by Peter Carlson. Even people who have neither read Clancy's novels nor seen the movies based on them recognize his name. It has been claimed that his books are the largest sellers in the world. Even if the statement is somewhat exaggerated, the numbers are right up there near the top. Whatever critical views, pro or con about the work, the accomplishment is notable.

Given the amount of time most writers struggle to attain a devoted readership, as well as financial success, Clancy's almost instant achievement of fame and fortune has impressed even cynical reviewers. Many of them refer to his earlier years when he only dreamed of becoming a writer but sold insurance to earn a living for his family. In "Isvestia—1" Clancy tells his audience he didn't find selling insurance "intellectually satisfying" (129), but when queried by television host Larry King about the number of years he spent in the insurance business, Clancy responds he wasn't smart enough to write earlier (24 Feb. 1995). As an agent he worked in Baltimore and Hartford until 1973. He and his family then moved to Owings, Maryland, where he worked for the O. F. Bowen Agency. After becoming a partner in the insurance business started and owned by his wife's grandparents, he bought the company in 1980. Both he and his wife continued in the business for some time after he achieved success as a writer, and it wasn't until 1987 that he retired from the agency.

He always wanted something different than the life of a businessman, even though he did well with 1,100 clients whose typical security needs he served. (That seems a large number until we learn that his publisher, Putnam, distributes Clancy's novels to about 11,000 bookstores in the United States alone.) Restless in the middle-class groove in which he found himself, he wanted what all inventive people long for, the kind of "immortality" produced by seeing something concrete. For writers it is seeing their name on book covers, and for Clancy it was also the dream of seeing books he had written in the Library of Congress. To satisfy his longing for excitement and creativity and his desire for fame he would carry home his typewriter every night. Seven nights a week he took over the family dining room table to work on his first novel. The first draft of *The Hunt for Red October* took him six months.

Like James Thurber's fictional Walter Mitty, to use Evan Thomas's description, Clancy "was a bored nobody," and as Clancy puts it "a nerd who reads books." He continues to talk of himself as "a nerd," a description he may have picked up from his father, who also went on using it after his son's success. Now it is altered to "a nerd who writes." Unlike Mitty, the unfulfilled dreamer, however, Clancy achieved much more than he had imagined. Thomas says he became "Walter Mitty for profit" (1988:61). In spite of the dedication and determination he'd had all the time he was writing, when he got a contract, finally finished *The Hunt for Red October*, and saw the book published, he didn't expect much to come of it. Although he'd received an advance of $5,000 from his first publisher, the Naval Institute Press, the success of the book caught him by surprise. Reminiscing about that, he tells various interviewers jokingly, that he'd have put sex in his book if he'd known he was writing a best-seller. Perhaps that accounts for the inclusion of some sex scenes in his recent novels. Although they might be considered mild in comparison with other thriller writers' descriptions, for Clancy they are fairly steamy.

Several people, including his usually practical wife, Wanda, were more optimistic than he about sales possibilities of his first book, but they did not anticipate the huge numbers. When Wanda read the manuscript, he asked her if she thought it would sell 5,000 copies. To his surprise, her response was, "More like 50,000" (Bennett 130). Still, in an interview for *American Legion Magazine*, Clancy claims that luck played a large part in his quick rise to best sellerdom. "I became a bestseller because Ronald Reagan read the book, told *Time* magazine he liked it, and Shazam, I got on the *New York Times* list" ("The Write Stuff":50). Having a president read that first book, admire it, and recommend it is as fortunate an occurrence as any writer could conceive. Clancy might have been a variation of Walter Mitty, but everything changed with his success. Suddenly everybody wanted to know him and be his friend.

How much was luck, how much change in the literary world, how much in the cultural and political climate would be impossible to measure. Clancy was fortunate in another way. As the director of the Naval Institute Press has pointed out, a major press would not have put as much effort into publicizing the novel. The Institute Press focused on the Washington market and that, combined with the glowing recommendation of President Reagan, proved to be the right strategy at the right time. Literary critics, analyzing Clancy's turn of fortune, frequently compare Reagan's "choice of light reading" to that of other presidents. They speak of Dwight Eisenhower's liking for the Western novels of Zane Grey and John Kennedy's for Ian Fleming's fictional spy, James Bond. Still, when Reagan's taste in fiction became public information, some critics expressed surprise over his selection of Clancy's work. One journalist asks, "What is there about this undersea chase fiction by a landlubbing insurance agent that so fascinates our current commander-in-chief—a man with access to most of the terrifying real military secrets in the world?" (Wainwright 7). The answer he gives to this particular question is twofold. Not only does the book provide escape from dreary reality, but also it reassures readers about the superiority of all things American. In other words, Clancy's *The Hunt for Red October* in many ways resembles Fleming's and most other escapist spy fiction. However, *Life* magazine's Loudon Wainwright goes further than simply seeing Clancy's work as formulaic. He calls that first novel a fantasy which is as close to "an act of propaganda and caricature as those scores of Happy Yank films Hollywood turned out during World War II" (7). Wainwright's views were not those of the majority of readers when Clancy burst on the publishing scene. Few reviewers assessed his work negatively. Such commentary was to come later.

Following the publication of *The Hunt for Red October* the then thirty-seven-year-old writer became "a literary phenomenon" (Cerasini 53). Readers wanted to know about him and soon learned he came from a background different from other popular writers of espionage fiction, most of whom have been British. Thomas L. Clancy, Jr., is an American of Irish descent. The second of three children, he was born in 1947, soon after his father returned from service in the navy. Although his own affection for the navy is clear, unlike some of the heroic characters in his novels he could not follow his father's pattern and join. Because the 6-foot-2, 180-pound, military-minded Clancy is myopic, he was rated 4F and rejected for military service during the Vietnam War. Aside from ROTC training at Loyola College, from which he was dismissed because of his poor eyesight, he has had no military experience.

Yet, the image created by the novelist is that of a military man. He wears darkly tinted aviator glasses and loves guns, ships, tanks, and planes (even though he is a nervous air passenger). He likes to dress in military style. A journalist meeting Clancy for a first-time interview describes his appearance: the clothing resembles a uniform, with "sharply pressed khaki pants, a dark-blue shirt" that has "the insignia of the U.S. Naval War College, an officer's parka over that and a gold-braided cap" with the words USS *Pharris* on it (Cooper 56). Nevertheless, this lover of all things military has been limited to fighting battles through computer games and the imagination. Because of his lack of actual experience in any branch of service or in combat, the type of writing he does has been faulted by some critics. Their judgments have annoyed him but have not influenced the work.

Military men are the writer's "kind of people" who "share the same value structure" (Hagman E2). They deserve much respect but do not get it from Congress or the news media, Clancy tells everyone, railing over lack of home support for military warriors who lose "because they were stabbed in the back by the politicians" (E. Thomas, 21 Aug. 1989: 60). The distaste he has for politicians, whom he finds less than honorable, is about equal to the affection Clancy holds for those in service. Because the military return his admiration, he has been rewarded with many adventures unavailable to other civilians. Admission to restricted bases, special tours of submarines, a week aboard a navy frigate, opportunities to drive an M-1 tank and fire its weapons all have come to him. His enthusiasm has led him to label some of these experiences as better than sex.[1]

As a result of his affinity to the military, the FBI, and the CIA he has been a frequent speaker for them. Occasionally he gives a speech as part of a barter arrangement. An example is a talk he delivered without charge at the Aberdeen Proving Grounds in exchange for trying out some new vehicles. Since Clancy normally gets paid well for speaking, he regards such bartering as fair trade. On the other hand, according to Peter Zimmerman, of the Carnegie Foundation for International Peace, the writer serves another purpose for the military. He has been used as "the authorized winked-at way to leak information that will help the military-procurement budget" (E. Thomas 1988:64). Nevertheless, Clancy has said again and again that he does not have access to classified material. Denial or not, now and then he has told interviewers in a somewhat vague manner that he is part of the "Great Chain," people in high places who help him out with information. Because of his high approval rating, said a Pentagon spokesman, "Everyone's willing to talk to Clancy" (Hixson 612).[2] Among his far-ranging supporters are Pentagon analysts who believe Clancy holds the same view of the world that they do. His positive portrayal of the nation and the military services, as well as his personal patriotism and that of his heroes, appeals to military leaders. Servicemen and women share the writer's belief in a powerful defense policy, endorsing his insistent view that we need to know everything about modern warfare to protect the country.[3]

Many readers could predict generally who Clancy's favorite people are. But interviewers often ask the writer to name specific people he admires. In response, he lists well-known figures in government or military positions, a director of the FBI, a director of the CIA. He names Congressman and Speaker of the House Newt Gingrich (Greenberg, "Interview"). Their respect is mutual. Gingrich, a former college professor, recommends Clancy's books to everyone in the belief that the novels will help people understand history. Also on Clancy's list of admirable people is General Colin Powell. Considering Clancy's support of actions in the Gulf War, Powell is an understandable choice. The novelist tells interviewer/editor Martin Greenberg that Powell is "the most impressive fellow I've ever met" (70).

Another military figure from a previous administration might have been included, but in the Greenberg interview, Clancy doesn't mention his name. (He does praise him strongly in other interviews.) That person is retired Colonel Oliver North, who also fits the writer's specifications of admirable public figures. Some of the beliefs Clancy shares with North are explored in *Without Remorse*. In fact, journalist Scott Shuger has declared that the novelist has the same ideas of the military as North, that his fantasies and military illusions are those of North, and that both are dangerous. The Irangate scandal that blemished the Reagan administration brought notoriety and fame to Colonel North. But because of his respect for Colonel North, Clancy, a Marylander, campaigned for him in Virginia in 1994. North, a former marine, was running on the Republican ticket for the Senate against Democrat Senator Charles Robb, also a former marine.

Clancy's support of candidates seems not to have helped them. His popularity as a writer has not influenced voters. Not only did Colonel North lose his bid for office, but so too did former Senator Helen Delich Bentley, who also got help from Clancy. Bentley ran in the Republican primary race for governor of Maryland but didn't make it through that first round of the election. Yet she and the novelist continue to share certain interests. Both have recently become unpaid members of the board of Monarch Avalon, Inc., a company that manufactures battle games. Clancy is a fan of strategy games, including one called Gettysburg. Meanwhile, following his defeat at the polls, Colonel North has gone on to host a radio talk show.

During and after his presidency, Ronald Reagan and his wife, Nancy, repudiated North, but in spite of that President Reagan and President Bush, both Republicans, always get high marks from the author. Talking with a journalist, Clancy stated he "wouldn't bet against George Bush on anything," because he "is just too damn good" ("The Write Stuff":

50). Clancy vigorously approves of the military activities of Reagan and Bush in Grenada and the Persian Gulf. However, he believes the United States should have gone further in the Gulf War by eliminating Saddam Hussein. He is less approving of Democratic administrations and has dubbed Democratic President Jimmy Carter "President Malaise" for not taking action at various times during his term in office (Ward 12).

The men named in the Greenberg interview often resemble characters in Clancy's novels, that is, military and government figures. In fact, some of his fictional portraits are so closely modeled after famous individuals that the reader might be able to identify them. There are, however, striking omissions from the list that provide insights into Clancy's thinking. Although Greenberg was limiting the scope by asking about "the public arena," other more far-ranging interviews have not produced a much different assortment of names.

No name from the arts world seems important enough to discuss in the Greenberg interview, compared to those in the government and military establishment, no painters, photographers, dancers, musicians, composers. They are almost never mentioned in any interviews nor in the novels, a somewhat surprising omission because Clancy developed a strong interest in art after buying his newest home. Under "Hobbies" in his 1995 Internet on-line biography he lists art and collecting first. Literature is fourth. In the Greenberg interview the novelist also ignores the names of other writers. Characters in his books, however, voice intense dislike of certain authors, usually nineteenth-century figures. Although Clancy was an English major at Loyola (graduating in 1969), he really doesn't like the word "literature," insisting it gives preferential status to specific types of work. In a number of instances he has been sarcastic about required readings in university courses and scornful about some "classics." He often speaks of himself as being "in the entertainment business," whereas "literature means a hundred years after you're dead they make kids read you in high school" (Anderson 85). Still, in a somewhat contradictory view, he wants to be regarded as more than an entertaining novelist.

On occasion, when asked directly about his favorite writers, Clancy has provided a very short list of contemporaries. Mainly these are thriller writers, among whom his favorite is Frederick Forsythe, his friend, and author of Clancy's favorite thriller, *Day of the Jackal*. At other times he has spoken of the science fiction writers he admires, H. G. Wells, Jules Verne, Jack London, Jack Williamson, Isaac Asimov. Also in that group, even though the work is "classic," he mentions Jonathan Swift's *Gulliv-*

er's Travels. Murder mysteries do not appeal to him. Neither does he like the novels of spy writers such as John Le Carré, whose work he considers morally ambiguous. There is never a question about Clancy's own moral stand.

No female names appear on Clancy's preferential lists of most admired people. If the matter arises, as it does often, he states flatly he knows little about women. Still, after publication of *Red October* Clancy noted that a third of his mail came from women readers. He is defensive or says little when questioned about his depiction—or the lack—of women in his work. Even if Clancy does not elaborate on distinctions he makes between male and female readers, the manner in which excerpts from his books appear does. A telling contrast exists between the presentation of two excerpts published in 1988, one in February in *Good Housekeeping* and one in August in *Popular Mechanics.* In *Popular Mechanics* the introductory blurb to the selection from *The Cardinal of the Kremlin* focuses on technology and an imaginary Strategic Defense Initiative (he rejects the term Star Wars) race between the United States and the Soviet Union. The lead-in is adapted to the male audience buying the magazine. On the other hand, the excerpt from *Patriot Games* appearing in *Good Housekeeping* is highlighted with the words "Romance! Suspense! Adventure!" (163). The drawings and the commentary attached to them, in what is considered a women's magazine, resemble material from books of an earlier era. It doesn't matter that terrorism and technology drive both these novels; the assumption is that women's interest in Clancy's fiction is only for romance. A word portrait of the Ryans in *Good Housekeeping* reads: "Jack and Cathy Ryan, both doctors, proud parents, and gorgeously in love" (164). Another is a drawing of Cathy Ryan in bed. Jack, leaning over her, says: "My breath stops when I think of you. Please . . . always love me back" (163–64). Even though Clancy is not the editor of either magazine and presumably has nothing to do with the layout, the presentation of each appears to be representative of his views of gender and readership. Aware of the discrepancies in his approach—and perhaps even with *Good Housekeeping* in mind—his supporters defend him. In his respectful analysis of *Patriot Games* in *The Tom Clancy Companion,* Marc Cerasini writes: "With *Patriot Games* Clancy set out to win female readers," but it was not "a calculated piece of commercial fluff" (25). This is also Clancy's view, if one is to believe the blurb on the cover of *The Companion.* It states that Clancy cooperated and approved of the material in the book, which gives the reader "a rare glimpse" into his mind.

Clancy's readers, in addition to the military, are all kinds of people at home and abroad. His novels are available in the most unexpected places; for example, in Pogradec, Albania, the largest public library of the Balkans has Clancy's fiction. The novels have been translated into ten or more foreign languages. In many parts of the world not only college graduates but blue-collar workers admire the work. Clancy himself comes from a working-class background, which he refers to proudly and frequently. His father, who died in March 1995, was a mail carrier, and to pay his annual $400 fee at Loyola High, his mother worked in the credit department at Montgomery Ward. Clancy points to his parents' modest income as his defense against statements that he scorns people who earn no more than $120,000 a year. When the question arose on *Larry King Live* (1993), Clancy denied having made such a comment. But *Washington Post* interviewer Peter Carlson had quoted Clancy as saying it. In the discussion that took place between Carlson and Clancy the novelist was proclaiming his familiar annoyance with Congress, something his readers recognize from the novels. Throughout his fiction Clancy frequently lambastes congressmen. Thus it should not be surprising to read in Carlson's report of their dialogue that Clancy spoke disdainfully about congressional activities, the incompetency of Congress, and his scorn for what he considers their limited salaries.

Characteristically, Clancy refers to money as a badge of success. When critics have reviewed him unfavorably, he has sometimes responded by pointing out the differences in his income and theirs. But, whether or not Clancy links money and the effectiveness of Congress, he has never been hesitant about his dislike of that body. His anger spills over when he talks to an admiring interviewer about congressional "wimp[ing] out . . . on everything." His perception that Congress does not support the military forces seems to provoke him more than anything else. Heaping scorn on congressmen, he makes a hyperbolic remark: "There are a lot of people in Congress who . . . would rather trash the military than hug their own kids" (Cooper 60). During this same interview he heatedly attacks a former congressman as an "arrogant little bastard" and a "little prick." The reason—the congressman made jokes in front of a television camera on the floor of the House about the war in Grenada. Not only does the writer question the patriotism of such people, but he also doubts their intelligence and abilities. He has said that many members of Congress lack information necessary to do their jobs, and he shows no hesitation in labeling many of them as failures.

One senator he admires is Daniel Patrick Moynihan of New York.

Since Moynihan is a member of the Democratic party, the "other party," the author's choice is unexpected. However, it does support his statement that he holds both conservative and liberal views. People who classify Clancy as a hawk are sometimes surprised to learn that he stands to the center or even left of center on certain issues. During the baseball strike of the 1994–95 season, Clancy, part-owner (one fourth) of the Baltimore Orioles, declared himself pro-union and on the side of the players. Agreeing with the major club owner (one-half), Pete Angelos, Clancy did not want to replace the team because he believes in the integrity of the game. When he told this to television host Larry King, who expressed some surprise, Clancy followed it up by saying he was once a teamster (24 Feb. 1995). A different interview reveals he also had worked one summer as a plumber.

Although in general the military rates the writer's accuracy very highly, a few dissenters say he makes them look too good to be realistic. According to that perspective, flesh and blood soldiers do not perform like those in novels. Neither do weapons. There are mistakes and casualties in actual battles. Clancy retorts that he always downgrades the efficacy of weapons from the claims of the manufacturers and that he takes pride in and is praised for his wide knowledge of weaponry. Contrary to news stories about some disappointments and failures in weapons systems during the Gulf War, Clancy claims reporters called to commend him about the accurate descriptions in his novels.

At various times, because of his strongly expressed views about politics and politicians, a number of people, including Republican political strategist Edward Rollins, have advised the novelist to run for office. Stating that his children are too young for him to take on a political career, he has always refused. Children reveal the soft and tender side of the writer, who holds what he labels "the Warrior's Code." Its most important rule is that "the strong . . . protect the weak" ("Turn Back": 149). The sentimental part of his nature surfaces with any suffering of children. In "Turn Back" he tells of his brief and painful, but uplifting relationship with a six-year-old boy who had cancer. The child, a fan, had written to him. Affected by the knowledge of the youngster's terminal condition, Clancy attempted to find things to interest him. He sent souvenirs, letters, videos, and arranged a tour of the USS *Dallas*. But he went further, giving a greater gift, that of time, when he spent four days with the boy in a tour of Disneyland.

In the light of such actions it isn't surprising that the writer would consider his family's needs before those of the public. Yet Clancy can seem contradictory. Although he has always said that his young children came first, some question might be asked about motivation. As with some other areas of his philosophy, Clancy can seem cynical and materialistic. Has he used the family as an excuse to just say no, or are his reasons more complex? When he spoke to a group of young scholars during National Education Week in 1990, Clancy "excoriated public service." Equating devotion to public service with "self-serving" politics, he advised the Presidential Scholars to have the independence of wealth before taking on any service to the country. Being rich is better than being poor, he told the audience of students and parents, and wealth protects one from the pressures that burden public figures (Wile 29).

Yet, he has often said that people like himself are needed in government. Because of that opinion he tried out the waters when he agreed to a request by then Vice-President Dan Quayle, a longtime admirer, to serve on a presidential commission. Its charge was deliberation about the future of space programs, and Clancy as an ardent supporter of the program was invited to participate. The vice-president's concern over the waning of public enthusiasm for space undertakings led to the formation of the commission, and he believed Clancy's involvement would be a boon to the Space Agency. However, the results were anything but good. Clancy and members of the commission didn't get along. Numerous stories about the confrontations, all different, surfaced from the group. Clancy thought most of the experience a waste of his time, but he also asserted that he was effective and useful in bringing about a change in leadership. Other members have been harsh in their evaluations of the novelist. Some comment specifically that he takes undeserved credit for subsequent events, but the general opinion is he doesn't allow points of view different from his own. According to Wanda Clancy, her husband is a man who "likes to be in charge. If he says something and he feels it makes sense, he wants to see it done" (Alson and Phillips 88).

Clancy continues to hold a deep interest in space. In one essay he poses the costs of social programs against those of space. Decrying budget cuts to the space program, he proposes that money spent on social changes should be given instead to the National Air and Space Agency (NASA). Although his opposition to welfare, various social reforms, and aid to the poor surfaces at various times in his novels, in "Back to the Frontier" it is undisguised. Pessimistically, he states there is little hope for improvement in the condition of the poor. They "may always be with us" as they have always been (115). Our future lies in space, he writes, looking toward what might be and what he believes should be the future.

Though critical, he offers no substitute plans for social change. In his novels, his irritation with government policies reveals itself when he suggests that people on welfare sometimes rip off the system.

His anger at waste in public spending extends to the issue of public education in the United States. Clancy prefers private to public schools. Although he does not limit the choice to Catholic or any other parochial schools, in novel after novel someone thinks or voices approval of Catholic school education. Graduates of Catholic colleges and universities are shown as superior in many subjects. Clancy's heroes know more than others about ethics and logic, perhaps even history. (Major characters in the novels always are better educated in history than others, and these players are always the product of Catholic education.) The writer, who has an abiding interest in history, prides himself on his knowledge of it. Clancy's own education has been in Catholic institutions, grammar school, high school, and college, all in Baltimore, Maryland. He is convinced that his strong value system comes from his parochial school background. However, he never says that American children must be sent to exclusively Catholic schools. What he does stress is his belief that private schools are superior to public schools. In support of that idea he points to the sacrifices some inner-city parents make to educate their children in private schools. Competition between both systems, he claims, would inevitably lead to an improvement in public school education. Competition, rather than increased funding, is the solution to the problem.

Clancy's mastery of science and technology and the brilliance behind his presentations would seem to belie his rueful evaluation of himself as a lazy and foolish student in his youth. He is regretful that laxity in studying limited what he could do with his life. Because of that he could become neither a physician nor an engineer, professions he admires highly. However, he was then and is now a constant reader. As a youngster he "was always the first boy waiting at the curb" waiting for the bookmobile (Bennett 128). The reading, of course, served him well in his ultimate career as writer. Now, in addition to watching CNN and Jim Lehrer for television news, he reads books, two daily newspapers, and several magazines. Preferring specialized magazines to general ones, he follows *Science News, Aviation Week, Space Technology,* and *Defense News.* In his house his study is filled with reference books that reveal his interests. *Jane's Fighting Ships: The Standard Reference of the World's Navies, Ships and Air Craft in the U.S. Fleet, Guide to the Soviet Navy,* and *Combat Fleets of the World* have served as central reference tools in his writing.

He maintains that technical data in many of his books comes from these sources. *Principles of Surgery* provides information that can be used in the descriptions of his numerous medical characters, the most important being Jack Ryan's wife, Cathy, an ophthalmic surgeon. At various times the writer describes her work in specific detail, always with textbook accuracy. And when she is awarded prizes, they are real, not invented by the author.

Not unexpectedly, another work found on the author's bookshelf is *Gun Digest*. Clancy delights in and owns all kinds of guns. Having learned to shoot as a youngster in a Boy Scout troop, he has made it one of his major hobbies in adulthood. But, as he stresses, shooting is just that, a hobby. He doesn't hunt, nor is he a member of the National Rifle Association. To Clancy owning a gun is a matter of individual freedom, a constitutional right. His view is the familiar one that people, not guns, hurt people. As long as a person does no harm, he should be permitted to possess firearms, Clancy states. Furthermore, drunk drivers pose more hazards to the public than gun owners. To support that point, in his essay "But I *Like* to Shoot" he notes that so law-abiding is he, he has never even had a speeding ticket.

The lack of discipline that plagued him as a student does not carry over to other areas. Even though the author speaks of himself as a lazy slob, he is tremendously disciplined when it comes to his writing. Going to work at his desk after breakfast, he spends five hours each morning working and generally writes about five pages in that time. His resoluteness is evident. In the ten-year period between 1984 and 1994, Clancy published eight novels, two nonfiction technological books (*Submarine* and *Armored Cav*), and numerous short pieces. It seems almost a rite of August to have a Tom Clancy novel appear, though he announced well in advance that 1995 would be different. On *CBS This Morning* (18 Aug. 1994), when he was asked by host Harry Smith whether he might be taking a vacation from writing, Clancy's response was "A writer writes."

Unlike other years, the summer of August 1995 saw no Clancy novel. Clancy did publish two nonfiction works in 1995: *Fighter Wing* and *Reality Check: What's Going On Out There?* But he is not retiring as a novelist. Questioned by Larry King about future writing plans, he replied, "Jack [Ryan] will be back" (24 Feb. 1995). Some time ago, musing about the future of Ryan, Clancy thought he might get to be president. In the conclusion to his most recent novel, *Debt of Honor*, the writer seems to be preparing the reader for just that situation.

Although often he has voiced something all authors know, that writing is very hard work, he has also called it great fun. Like his readers, Clancy gains pleasure from discovering the story as it goes along. For that reason, he says, he does not use outlines. Marc Cerasini questions Clancy's statement, basing his skepticism on his reading of *Red October* and *Patriot Games*. References in *Red October* to episodes in *Patriot Games* suggest planning, according to Cerasini. But others might see it differently inasmuch as Clancy has told some interviewers he wrote *Patriot Games* first, although it was published after two other books. It is likely that events from *Patriot Games* were in his mind when he turned to a different kind of story but one in which he used the same hero. Even if he does not work from an outline, the author sees most of his fiction as a series and has an overview of direction. He claims he is never more than one book ahead. He doesn't like multiple book contracts, only one at a time.

Because he thinks of himself as a storyteller, for Clancy as for most storytellers, the interest is not in the style of the telling. It is in the telling itself, the plot, and the characters. Aware of the criticism of his prose style, on occasion he says he is working on it. At other times he is defensive and angry, because what he is attacked for by some critics he is praised by others. Not unexpectedly, his editor, Neil Nyren, praises his instincts and calls him a "terrific craftsman" (Hagman E2). From the beginning, however, all critics have commended him for the extraordinary amount of research but not for his writing ability.

Although, reviewers were in general kinder about his prose in the early years, even then some found it only serviceable. They have grown harsher with time. Most reviewers now accuse him of explaining too much, of overwriting, though most agree he is outstanding in his ability to pull all the parts of plots together. Movie critics usually like the films made from Clancy's fiction, but not the originals. One reviewer, praising a movie to the detriment of the novel, calls Clancy "the most eminently skimmable of modern popular novelists" (Hinson D1). The books are too long, there are too many plots, the machinery is more interesting and more complex than the characters, book and movie critics write. They describe a great sameness among the characters, as if they are stamped from a mold. Only a few book critics have found his characters attractive, whereas movie critics laud only those on the screen.

In spite of the success of the movies based on his work, Clancy has gone to war with Hollywood. The dislike is mutual. Each camp has issued derogatory statements about the other. The author's unkindest cut is to compare people in Hollywood to those running government agencies. Angered by the changes made in translating his novels to films, the author thinks his work has been emasculated, and he has protested loudly and long. Even though he did not write the scripts, he continued to criticize the movies, claiming the integrity of his work is at issue. In Hollywood Clancy's quarrelsomeness led to difficulties significant enough to be reported in the national newspapers. During the filming of *Patriot Games* he was described as disruptive, a man given to "temper tantrums." He bombarded the studio with memos, which Clancy himself said were as many as "14 pages, single spaced" (Cox A6). Since Hollywood first began making movies, other novelists have been as unhappy as Clancy with the rewriting of their work, among them, Isaac Bashevis Singer with *Yentl* and William Faulkner with several novels. Most authors recognize they have given up their rights of control once a contract has been signed. Clancy, however, has been less compliant. Because of his anger over the changes to his novels, he has chosen an independent company to make his 1993 novel, *Without Remorse*, and when it is made, he will be involved with the production. He emphasizes that he wants control of his work.

In the interim, between the release of his next book and the movie based on *Without Remorse*, Clancy has turned to television, though it may be only a brief hiatus. Through that medium, in February 1995, he brought together a suspense novel and filmscript. If the plan had been to show a strong Clancy hand in the making of a movie, it failed. Reviewers gave the show an unusual amount of coverage, and in the process most damned the entire program. Although the paperback book and the program are called *Tom Clancy's Op Center*, the fine print reveals otherwise. *Op Center* was "created by Tom Clancy and Steve Pieczenik." "Created" is the key term, because the novel, whose plot differs from the television script, had a ghostwriter, named Jeff Rovin (Mansfield, 27 Feb. 1995:B1).

The film, says television reviewer Tom Shales, was "adapted from the novel Clancy didn't write by . . . [scriptwriter] Steve Sohmer." In other words, Clancy wrote neither the novel nor the film script, but his name on both guaranteed them an audience. Shales flays the film, calling it "old rubbish" intended "to exploit the pathetic pseudo-machismo of infantile armchair warriors." He finds it "laughable. . . . a joke," proving his evaluation through mockery of the style. Using the word "meanwhile" six times, he humorously recreates the idea behind the frantic scene shifts, which are supposed to deliver suspense. Since frequent shifts of scene are a Clancy signature in the novels, the script writer of

"Op Center" must have thought such shifts would also be thrilling television fare. Shales finds them ridiculous, and he scolds Clancy for putting his name on a book and film he didn't write. Shales advises the novelist to be "the tiniest bit original and imaginative." Then, striking his final blow, he concludes: " 'Tom Clancy's Op Center' is really 'A Farewell to Brains' " (26 Feb. 1995:G5–6). With reviews like that it is not likely there will be the series of "Op Center" productions that the novelist had contemplated.

Unlike Clancy's novels, "Op Center" was disparaged for everything—plot, style, and characters. In reviewing the novels, most critics have applauded the plots, though they have often been lukewarm about the style and frequently faulted the writer's characterization. Adverse reactions to his characters arouse Clancy's wrath more than criticism of his prose or plots. He defends his characterizations vigorously, pointing out he has been praised for his accuracy by Russian, British, and American military men. Scornful of reviewers who find his characters unbelievable, he informs them that the people who really know, those who are "insiders in the business," find characterizations his great strength (Ward 12).

Although one journalist states that Clancy's heroes are usually "Irish Catholic cops and soldiers" (E. Thomas 1989:60), the range is somewhat broader than that. Irish Catholic, yes, most of the time. Yes to cops sometimes, and yes to soldiers (and sailors and marines), if the prefix "ex" were also added. His major figure, Jack Ryan, served briefly in the marines before moving on to other activities. So too with John Kelly/Clark (a former navy SEAL), the action-driven "dark" hero who appears in almost as many books as Ryan, though generally in a supporting role. Ding Chavez, the Mexican-American army hero of *Clear and Present Danger*, also becomes ex-military when recruited for the CIA by Clark, who was himself recruited years before.

As for villains, there is much of a sameness, as well. Often they are "patrician WASPs and devious foreigners" (E. Thomas 1989:60). Occasionally, however, even foreigners are good people. Perhaps "good guys" should be used because Clancy likes it so much, saying, "that's the way cops talk." Furthermore, it is the way the writer thinks "in a lot of cases" (Cooper 161). For foreigners to be "good guys" they usually have to be high-minded enough to understand the superiority of the West. They must be willing to risk their lives to save their country, or perhaps even the world. Some of them betray their country in order to save it.

Americans who commit treason, however, can never be "good guys," no matter what lofty sentiments they proclaim. Usually the novelist portrays them as super-liberal white Anglo-Saxon Protestants (WASPs) who, by virtue of birth, have been given everything desirable. They have money, education (at Ivy League schools), family connections that get them good jobs, and influence. Characteristically, they are self-centered and indifferent to human life. They lack the ability to reason logically, so that while they are class conscious, they are also swept along by any "politically correct" idea. Some take drugs. Several are homosexual, perhaps driven to treason by sexual needs and entrapped by those passions. The writer's often harsh portrayal of homosexuals fits one description of him as "an unapologetic homophobe" (E. Thomas 1988:61). Clancy makes no effort to disguise his antagonism either in his books or in conversation. During the Bush administration, the author asserted that he thought two of Defense Secretary Richard Cheney's aides should be dismissed because they were homosexual ("The Write Stuff":51). When journalists have asked about his views of homosexuals in the military, his response also is negative, making it clear that his is the position of the men in service. Although the major or minor heroes of the novels do not discuss sexual preference, disgust for lifestyles different from their own comes through in a variety of ways.

Peter Carlson has found a "vague resemblance" between Clancy's name and those of his heroes. The resemblance usually comes from the Irish heritage, though sometimes the sound of the name reminds us of the author's. On a number of occasions, Clancy has spoken of superhero Ryan as a "new improved version" of himself. Ryan's beliefs are Clancy's. "If it's Jack Ryan's thoughts or the words of the narrator, it's probably me saying something I happen to believe in," Clancy tells Martin Greenberg (65). Although it is not considered wise to conclude that characters speak for an author, in Clancy's novels whoever the major character is, he serves as spokesman for Clancy. Thus, even when Kelly/Clark, the dark and violent hero takes center stage, the reader may safely assume his beliefs also are Clancy's. Those beliefs have been described as inflexible and conservative, although the writer claims he has grown more moderate as he has become more successful. He is a "law-abiding" and "fair" man, and he "believes in the system," says Marc Cerasini (who has his own doubts about the way things are). Still, Cerasini notes, Clancy suggests in *Clear and Present Danger* that due process may no longer be affordable, in spite of our greater need for it today (43). The later novel *Without Remorse* further explores failures in government and law, which are "corrected" by heroic men and acts.

Both major heroes, Ryan and Clark, express their views (and Clancy's) openly, and although Clark is a more physical type who never hesitates to act, both men are take-charge figures. Clancy has said he wasn't trying to develop a James Bond figure in Ryan. Undoubtedly he would deny any resemblance between the two; yet the reader may find numerous instances where Ryan's deering-do looks much like that of Bond. That is even truer of John Clark, who sometimes seems a combination of Bond, Batman, and Superman—Clark Kent/John *Clark*. Even characteristics of cartoon figures (and their names) have a place in the fiction. Similarities do not mean the writer consciously set out to make his characters look like those favorites of the public. All writers are influenced in their development by the books they have read as well as film and television fare. People who write thrillers are also readers of thrillers who have absorbed numerous traits of earlier thriller writers.

Ryan has strong detractors as does Bond, though Ryan's critics are more numerous. Whereas the worst comment about Bond labels him a fool, Ryan is compared to a machine, a man who "personifies . . . mechanical perfection" (Shuger 16). His hierarchy consists of God, guns, and country, in that order (Carcaterra 32). One reviewer describes Ryan as "the very model of a Yuppie officer and gentleman" (Lehman 68). Since the use of the term "yuppie" generally carries an air of disapproval, the reader can only guess at the underlying point. Is Ryan too ambitious? Too rich? Too power hungry? Yet, with all that, a gentleman?

Although Cerasini sees the Ryan family—Jack, Cathy, and the children—as American "society in *microcosm*" (27), on reflection, many readers would disagree with him. The only real similarity is in family structure, that is, mother, father, and children. Cathy and Jack are young, attractive multimillionaires, who live in a multimillion-dollar house, drive several top-of-the-line cars, have outstanding occupations, and are admired by the entire world. They are always moving up, always in charge, always winning prizes, awards, gifts, praise. Do most readers agree with Cerasini? Or, are they more like reviewer Janet Maslin, who finds Cathy Ryan "the wise, smiling, insufferable wife" (3 Aug. 1994: C16). Isn't Cathy a fantasy wife, as much as her husband is a fantasy figure for readers? Thrillers, after all, satisfy multiple needs in the audience. They don't want people like themselves, but characters who fulfill their secret fantasies—the perfect woman, the rich and powerful man, the always-splendid children.

Many critics, however, do not read Clancy's novels in the way they read most thrillers and therefore do not apply the same standards to their judgments of his work. Evaluations of the novelist's fiction have run the gamut from "dangerous" to praising the service it has done for the world. Clancy reacts strongly to those who depreciate his work, describing critics as people "who can't write and hate(s) anyone who can" (Thomas 1988:64). His sense of injury is not unique. Authors always feel stung by harsh reviews. Yet, in spite of Clancy's many favorable reviews, he has also had some very bad press. In part it may be because he, with the help of others, appears to have set himself up as a pundit. Being asked by a president, a vice-president, high-ranking military officials, and even some newspeople (after the April 1995 bombing in Oklahoma) for his views and help is heady stuff. Over the course of a decade he has become more than a novelist for much of the public. And as he has gained recognition, he has changed, at least in the eyes of some journalists, who didn't see what one reviewer did, the "considerable ego" underneath "the sporadic modesty" (Anderson 85).

In a 1988 interview the novelist was described as modest, unassuming, and disarmingly funny (Cooper 56), although in earlier years some critics had found him uncomfortable, nervous, and reticent. Chameleonlike, he soon lost his reticence. Success provided a comfort zone, but, as he assured journalists, it didn't change him. Interviewers wrote and spoke of his friendliness, his spontaneity and quick humor. No longer. Even though his television appearances belie the hostile statements he is reported to have made, now he is described by critics as short-tempered, prickly, impatient, and arrogant. If an interviewer doesn't use such words, he may choose quotes that say them for him. Recently Clancy's personality has seemed almost as much a subject of review as his work.

Only time will tell whether the fact that in the last two years Clancy's work has become the butt of humor will affect its popularity in any way. Such humor, after all, attests to the fact that almost everyone knows Clancy's name and recognizes his face. Do faithful readers care that columnist Tony Kornheiser, in his lighthearted description of insensitivity in men, writes: "Men don't understand subtlety. That's why they read books by Tom Clancy" (F1)? Kornheiser has poked fun at Clancy's work at various times, as have some other critics, but the writer who has been winning the war of humor is Christopher Buckley. It began when Buckley wrote a witty and unflattering review of Clancy's *Debt of Honor* and simultaneously branded him as the most successful bad writer of the era ("Megabashing Japan"). Clancy's numerous belligerent responses to the review only fired up Buckley's wit. When he is angry, Clancy loses his normally funny touch. Buckley, a humorist, doesn't. In what has become repetitious, Clancy compares the large amount of money he makes from his books to what Buckley gets from his, but that doesn't ruffle Buckley.

One instance of Buckley's mockery of Clancy's novels came in December of 1994 when the *Washington Post* "Book World" printed a special section called "If Your Life Were a Book." A number of authors were called on to imagine what might be, among them Christopher Buckley, whose choice of answers was to say he wanted Tom Clancy to write his (Buckley's) life story. Taking the opportunity to spoof Clancy's subject matter and prose style, he invents a situation in which he burlesques Clancy's writing. Buckley, presumably pretending to be a Jack Ryan type, hears from the president of the United States, "You are the most manliest man this country ever produced" (8). A week later, in his column for the *New Yorker* (12 Dec. 1994:136), Buckley writes a spoof of imagined programs for a new conservative cable channel. The Buckley programs, of course, are ludicrous, and as he makes fun of many well-known figures, he doesn't spare Clancy. He puts Clancy in an imaginary late-night slot called "The Great Books—Tom Clancy talks about how he has grown as a writer." To the author and his serious-minded readers this might not seem a joke—because they believe it to be true—but to Buckley and his readers it is a lark.

Clancy's fame and financial success are attested to in many ways: his large sales in other languages; his appearance in an ad for American Express, which uses only celebrities of high visibility. And also, in an *Esquire* picture article ("How the Other Half Writes"), there is his grouping with some of the biggest sellers of the day. Those shown, in addition to Clancy, are Jackie Collins, Anne Rice, Sidney Sheldon, Danielle Steele, Evan Hunter (also known as Ed McBain), Father Andrew Greeley. The introductory description states that the featured writers are neither "Stendhal [n]or Virginia Woolf" ("The Literary Life: How the Other Half Writes," *Esquire*, July 1989:82). Such a line suggests the writers are all lightweights, entertainers, but rich and successful ones. Surely that is not how Clancy sees himself, and it is surprising, if he knew in advance about it, that he would allow himself to be included in that particular company. He has complained frequently that thriller writers are not taken seriously (seeming not to have heard of the stir several of John Le Carré's books made in newsrooms). And, ironically, in a *Time* article that appeared a month before the one in *Esquire,* Walter Shapiro wrote that Clancy "should not be dismissed as merely another book-biz commodity, the action-adventure counterpart to Danielle Steele or Sidney Sheldon" (67). One has to wonder whether there is a split vision, each at odds with the other, the issue of money and success versus seriousness and influence?

Clancy's life, like that of few other figures in American literary history, reads as if it were a Horatio Alger book—good, deserving, hardworking young man is rewarded with all he seeks. He is "the American Dream come true," says interviewer Cynthia Ward (5). He and his admirers look back at how far he has come. Along with his older sister and younger brother he grew up in a very modest home in Baltimore, in a happy, conservative, and religious family. Young Tom, his namesake, was close to his father. The senior Clancy, an amateur baseball player, who loved the sport, coached Little League teams. Love of the game was passed from father to son, but the younger Clancy lacked his father's skills. When the novelist bought an interest in the Orioles Baseball Team in 1993, he hoped to take his father to the games. To the author's everlasting regret his father suffered several strokes and died before that could happen.

Clancy credits his father for stressing the importance of independence. The values he learned at home and in parochial school remained even as his lot changed dramatically. In August 1969, when he married Wanda Thomas, a nursing student, they also moved to a modest home, a three-bedroom, one-bath rambler that was barely adequate as their family expanded. Both Tom and Wanda worked out of her parents' house in the insurance business. Once his early novels provided the money for a move in 1986, it was to a five-bedroom with library, split-level, $200,000 house in Prince Frederick County in southern Maryland. The novelist no longer had to carry his IBM Selectric from office to home and back again. He could afford a computer, and he was thinking of hiring a secretary because of the volume of mail. He purchased the car he'd dreamed of, a Mercedes Benz—the price given ranges from $39,000 upward to the fifties—and bought the watch that proclaims success, a Rolex. Nevertheless, he informed a newsman, he was still drinking "discount sherry and chang[ing] diapers" (Levine 66).

The diaper-changing days and the drinking of discount sherry came to an end. However, the writer has taken pains to point out to interviewers that he, his wife, and their four children—Michelle, Christine, Tommy, and Katie—continue to prefer the simple things in life. They often eat in the kitchen. It's still McDonald's and bacon cheeseburgers after a long trip and too much foreign food. Church on Saturday night, and then McDonald's. Since moving from their second to their third house they have had plenty of household help, including a nanny, a housekeeper, and a caretaker. The new house is located in Huntington, Maryland, on the Chesapeake Bay, forty miles from Washington. Overlooking the water, the house sits on top of a sandstone cliff on Clancy's eighty-acre estate. Named Peregrine Cliff, duplicating the name of hero Jack Ryan's home, it has many similar features, although as the novelist points out, as if in competition with Ryan, his is the larger house. (Several journalists have suggested that Clancy identifies so strongly with Ryan that he even craves the jobs his character has held. Clancy also compares the ten-million-dollar fortune of Jack Ryan to his own. Clancy has surpassed that.) Many features of the house and grounds seem to come from the novels—the sandstone cliff, the view of the bay, the modern, multilevel house with "marvelous" woodwork (*Patriot Games* 483)—red oak in the novelist's home. What he dreamed for his hero, the novelist has given himself, but more.

"Clancyland," the term conferred by journalist Peter Carlson on the novelist's estate, has everything anyone could dream of or want. The 15,000-square-foot stone mansion that many visitors call "fortresslike" is so overwhelming that Clancy's father said, "You have to drop bread crumbs so you don't get lost" (Alson and Phillips 87). Guarded by dark gray electronically controlled security gates, the house is reached after a half-mile drive taking one past acres of lawn, flowers, shrubs, basketball courts, tennis courts, and a football field. Sitting on the lawn is the item that has caught the attention of everyone who has seen it, a World War II tank, a Christmas present from the novelist's wife. (Clancy has a passion for tanks.)

A marble entrance hall leads into a family room with a cathedral ceiling, a large stone fireplace, and an extensive view of Chesapeake Bay. That room, with its dark green leather upholstered chairs and family mementos, was furnished first. The residence of twenty-four rooms, some twenty by thirty feet, has sixteen-foot ceilings, floors covered with oriental rugs, walls covered with paintings, and fresh flowers everywhere. Wraparound decks overlook the bay, but there is no Clancy-owned boat, because Wanda Clancy doesn't like them. The bay can be seen through the large expanse of glass in every room of the house except the dining room. Even the above-ground basement has a glass wall with a water view. An upstairs office/library contains a billiard table, shelves filled with 3,000 books, catalogues, hats, caps, and helmets. A tank shell three feet high is the ashtray for the two packs of Merit Extra Lite cigarettes the author smokes each day, though he is always planning to give up smoking. Connected to his office by a spiral staircase is a secretarial office below, crowded with photographs of celebrities. The Clancy house has every kind of "toy," every kind of hardware, from games to gadgets. Included are "four personal computers, six phone

shooting war are at the heart of *Without Remorse*. Economic war is related to actual warfare in *Debt of Honor*. Furthermore, Clancy's pages are brimming over with death and responsibility, elements that Harper considers essential. In all Clancy's work, violence in some form brings on death to large or small groups of people. Responsibility for hostile acts is always clear, so that the reader knows from the start where the blame lies, and it is never with "us"—the "good guys."

Clancy's novels, like most popular thrillers, have certainty in them. A single-minded philosophy puts the United States, its military, and pre-selected individuals in the good category and the opposition in the bad. No shades of gray are sketched in. Although Clancy's world is technologically complex, his "friendly forces" characters, as well as the private and public world they live in, are not. They are "our" people, knowable and dependable. We can count on them to bring about justice as we understand it.

The heroes of Clancy's fiction risk their lives in the manner of medieval knights, even though at first nothing signals their special qualities. They may prefer to stay at home in a safe environment, doing familiar, enjoyable work, but when duty requires something else, they do it bravely. Toland in *Red Storm Rising* is an example. Ryan, the major Clancy hero, may be terrified of flying, but he does it anyway, just as he automatically risks his life again and again in dangerous situations. Ryan behaves that way from the moment he is introduced in *Red October* and on through each successive novel. There are also examples of ordinary, decent men who do not seem at first to have any of the makings of a hero. Yet, when events test them, they become leaders of men and saviors of women. Edwards, the meteorologist in *Red Storm Rising*, is that type of man. He would rather die than be a James Bond who secretly thrills to the idea of "the tang of rape" (*Casino Royale:* 157). Clancy's heroes do not have such thoughts. They are men set apart from others, superior to those around them. Nevertheless, almost always they work within the establishment.

Jack Ryan, though individualized in memorable ways, comes through the traditional line of thriller novels and is an amalgam of traits of prior figures. Like sleuths and agents of early suspense fiction, Ryan has not chosen as his vocation any form of secret or investigative work, but it finds him. Although he differs from the low-key hero of some of the 1920s–30s Golden Age English detective, he does have a number of resemblances. (It is not surprising that we think of English figures, for both author and his hero show great affection for all things English.) The famed English writer Dorothy Sayers's Lord Peter Wimsey, for example, is rich, intelligent, well educated, a university graduate. He served and was injured in World War I, is an amateur sleuth but plays a role in government intelligence. Jack Ryan is also rich, well educated, successful even when he least expects it, a failure at nothing, a former marine, and involved in intelligence. In yet another bow to the English heroes, Clancy has the queen reward an exploit of Ryan's by dubbing him Sir Ryan.

When introduced in Clancy's first thriller, Ryan thinks of himself as an average citizen, a teacher/scholar. Of course the experienced thriller reader knows and expects him to be anything but average. With each book Ryan becomes more like the superstars of other thriller novels. He soon gives up his enjoyable teaching position to work for the CIA, and his exploits begin to rival those of any thriller hero. Not only does he place himself in harm's way but unwittingly does the same with his family. Family attachments also put him in greater danger. In *Patriot Games* when wife Caroline (Cathy) and daughter Sally are seriously injured by terrorists seeking vengeance on Ryan himself, he takes actions that he would not have followed had they not been attacked. Like other thriller heroes he refuses to let the law do all the work, and he throws himself into the center of action. He wins out, but there is a price, and over time, that is, over a ten-year series of novels, he changes. The quiet, cool-headed man of the first book becomes secretive, extremely active, and even explosive as he ages. With each novel we also see a more cynical Ryan, the result of his exposure to evil men and philosophy.

THE SPY NOVEL

Another applicable description of Clancy's work is "spy novel." Lest someone protest that Clancy is not a spy writer, we have only to consider LeRoy Panek's judgment that a work is a spy novel if there is a single spy in it. Furthermore, that view is bolstered by Marc Cerasini's essay in *The Tom Clancy Companion*. In writing about "the birth of a genre," Cerasini describes Clancy's fusion of "military fiction with near-future apocalyptic science fiction, touches of espionage fiction, and a large dose of social realism" (25). Those "touches of espionage fiction" in Clancy's work require consideration of the features of spy stories if we are to place it completely.

Critics assign different dates to the "first" or most important British spy novel, which is the true ancestor of American espionage fiction, even though occasionally someone will name the American James Fenimore Cooper's *The Spy* (1821) as the earliest example of the genre. Historians have said spying came about as early as the Middle Ages. Nevertheless, actual spies did not have the romantic aura that fiction conferred on them with the development of the spy novel in the nineteenth century. Scholars agree that spy stories are linked to the Industrial Revolution, which occurred in Great Britain and parts of Europe before the United States. As Britain became highly industrialized, its weaponry, naval power, and eventually its airplanes were seen as a threat, as well as a source of envy to foreign powers. Spying took on an important role in reality and in fiction.

Modern thriller/espionage writers (as well as detective story writers) are indebted to a number of nineteenth-and early twentieth-century authors who created the form. According to some scholars, the prolific novelist William LeQueux is said to have provided the major guidelines of the spy novel, in spite of the unreadability of most of his work. LeQueux's importance to the development of espionage fiction also comes through what Panek calls his "pseudo-histories." These resemble war prophecy novels and argue "for military preparedness" (8). Although LeQueux was writing at the turn of the nineteenth century, his indirect effect may be seen in later writers who in turn influenced Clancy. LeQueux's work also suffers from what Panek calls "the worst brand of Victorian sentiment" (9). Sentiment, however, is not unique to LeQueux. Inasmuch as he is hardly the only author whose novels become mired in embarrassing mawkishness, we can't trace that tendency in Clancy back to LeQueux alone.

Also among the forerunners of the modern spy novel is the work of E. Phillips Oppenheimer, which provided one particular type of motif we find in Clancy. That is Oppenheimer's variation on the war prophecy novel, "prediction of an averted war instead of an actual one" (Panek 18). Oppenheimer's spy fiction takes on issues common to both the war prophecy novel and the averted war novel, issues that Clancy makes use of also. Both novelists show concern about the sufficiency of defense, the strength and weaknesses of military preparedness, and secret weapons.

Most scholars agree that the first "good" spy fiction is a war prophecy novel, *The Riddle of the Sands*, written by Erskine Childers in 1903. Critic/novelist Julian Symons states it is that novel which established a double standard for spying. Enemy spies have evil motives, whereas "we" have only worthy intentions (234). (Depending on who the novelist is, the "we" may differ. In *Riddle of the Sands* it is the British, and in most spy fiction by English or American writers, their compatriots are the worthy "we.") Symons claims that the duality of the moral problem—we are good, they are bad—existed only through the first few decades of the twentieth century, coming to an end with the work of Eric Ambler. His position is belied not only by a reading of Clancy's novels but also by an examination of the varieties of fiction of the years following World War II.

The most important writer for our consideration of the "development of the spy novel or the detective novel" (and for examination of Clancy's relationship to them) is John Buchan. "The modern novel of espionage simply would not have developed along the same lines without him" (Panek 39). Even today his novels continue to exert their influence on mystery—spy/thriller/adventure novels, and "in its best manifestations the spy novel returns to him" (Panek 66). Even novelist John Le Carré tips his hat to the great earlier writer by using a Buchan title in one of his own books.

Like thrillers, all spy fiction is not the same. Several literary historians have called attention to two clear divisions in the spy fiction genre. One is in the heroic, conservative, traditional camp. The other is realistic and ironic, in the mode of modern fiction. The first, as defined by Symons, supports "authority," asserting "that agents are fighting to protect something valuable." He describes the other type as "radical, critical of authority," with claims "that agents perpetuate, and even create, false barriers between 'us' and 'them' " (243). Other critics note that the traditional archetypal form has more violence, as well as more vitality and hope than the later one. The earlier type generally has a happy and conclusive ending, much like the novels of the Victorian Age. All loose ends are tied, all issues settled, if only temporarily. The realistic spy novel with its antiheroes, its darkness, and sense of despair is much closer in tone to modern and postmodern thought. Not surprisingly, the spy novel that utilizes traditional motifs (even with updated variations) is the one that is most successful commercially even though it is the other type that literary pundits find more meaningful.

Clancy and the Spy Novel

By the 1980s the time was right for Clancy's unique blending of modes, the uniquely modern and the traditional. In traditional ways his work bears multiple resemblances to Buchan's. Both Buchan's novels and

Clancy's are realistic in their use of actual historical events, but both mix them with fabricated incidents. Buchan's chief character Richard Hannay is, like the later Jack Ryan, a series figure. The two, who look and sound like the typical English or American reader, are a meld of romantic and ordinary figure. Buchan's fiction is a form of "Victorian" schoolboy literature, that is, it focuses on adventure, morality, heroism, and friendship. These same characteristics, though updated, are central to Clancy's work. Also notable in Buchan's novels is "the absence of believable, complete women characters" (Panek 45). Though hardly a remarkable characteristic in any spy novels, it is another resemblance between Buchan and Clancy's fiction. Finally, one small link that seems appropriate to Buchan but somewhat entertaining in Clancy: Buchan's characters have memories of grouse shooting. Sir Jack Ryan also has such memories.

THE TECHNOTHRILLER

Critics combined the words technology and thriller into "technothriller" to give a more precise definition to another variation in genre. The term "thriller" by itself does not suggest the differences in technological fiction. Although there is much overlapping of characteristics, the technological novel has some distinctive traits of its own.

Technothrillers are not completely the product of the modern age but have become significant additions to popular literature with the phenomenal advance of technology in the second half of the twentieth century. Contemporary writers have made use of technology unknown before the Second World War. These technothriller novelists build their work around technology that is both current and projected or futuristic. Every manner of complex machines, usually real but sometimes imagined, is fodder for the work. The technothriller may focus on any area from ocean to outer space. It may concern all forms of nuclear weaponry, missiles, submarines, aircraft. Perhaps it foregrounds computers that reach beyond human ability to solve problems. Laboratories with scientists—biologists, chemists, physicists, archaeologists—study unknown and as yet unsolved questions of existence, DNA, germs, viruses, extinct species.

In addition to the resemblances of technothriller to thriller fiction, there is sometimes the reminder of SF, and not only in the futuristic element. Still, some important distinctions exist. Unlike SF, the technothriller world is earthbound although its machines go out into space. It is the world the reader knows, even if its complexities are baffling. It is not the estranged world of SF. Scholars point out that characters in technothrillers are usually less interesting than the technology. However, people in technothrillers are recognizable humans, different from the fantasized, imaginary, or robotics figures of SF.

Although people are necessary to put things into motion (the thriller aspect), the plot in a technothriller depends more on advanced technology than on human character. Technothrillers are often a form of military fiction, with players who are soldiers, sailors, pilots. The novel serves as a subordinate backdrop to display advancements and projections of weaponry and war. Actual war, possible war, or averted war is fought on the pages of the technothriller. However, war is not limited to mass destruction of a martial nature. There may be other kinds of war, perhaps a financial war, dependent on modern technology, which could destroy the world economy. The crises and solutions in most technothrillers are mechanical. People may make mistakes, but the focus of the plot is on the machinery not on human limitations. The "good" characters in technothrillers are clearly delineated, are on the "right" side and, in the military fiction, are superpatriots. Invariably, the cast of characters is large. Although there may be a single traditional hero, the wide scope of the playing field requires a great many people, so many in fact that often they seem as faceless as their machines.

Clancy and the Technothriller

No matter how much technology dominates his books, Clancy's basic formula comes from the thriller. The fact that he sees himself as a writer of political thrillers further emphasizes the point that the thriller model is the primary one he has followed. Yet, his fiction has some SF connections and is especially close to espionage novels in its inclusion of spies, and, as critic William Ryan calls them, "other mavens of espionage" (26). However, Clancy's enjoyment of gadgets, his early reading of SF stories, including those filled with gadgetry, his monitoring of scientific developments, his fascination with computers, his admiration for all things military, and his very strong sense of patriotism connect him to the technothriller.

Marc Cerasini provides some background for Clancy's work, by describing the fiction and films that preceded his novels. He tells of the changing attitudes of the second half of this century: "Traditional war novels, tales of personal heroism and self-sacrifice that reinforced higher values of social responsibility, the type of fiction characteristic of the years following the Second World War, were replaced with a fiction of cynicism and defeat" (7). Antiwar novels and movies became popular for a time, one result of the unpopularity of the Vietnam War. But, even during the war, SF writers were creating promilitary novels and cleverly disguised war films. Cerasini writes that "Star Wars" is really a "reincarnation" of "unabashedly patriotic films of the 1940s." Filmmaker George Lucas, claims Cerasini, made "the villains clear-cut fascists, the good guys honest and noble" (8). Similar films proved popular, and novels moved in the direction of technology and politics.

By the 1980s the time was ripe for the fiction of Clancy. All his novels employ technology, even *Patriot Games*, which the novelist considers a love story. Like the work of other technothriller writers, almost everything in Clancy's plots and their central episodes depends on advanced technology. For Clancy, like many other contemporary technothriller writers, that technology involves military matters. Because of that identification he has been described as "the novelist laureate of the military industrial complex" (R. Thomas 1).

His multiple characters are often flat and subordinate to the technology. Aside from his alter-ego character, Jack Ryan, and his other favorite, John Kelly (Clark), Clancy's people are types rather than individuals. Some reviewers also classify Ryan and Kelly that way, comments that anger the author greatly. He is exasperated by critics who describe his machines as more interesting, complex, and lifelike than his characterizations. He angrily defends his portrayal of characters. Even if he scoffs at the word "literature," and at critics, he wants to be known as a writer who understands everything about his creations. In his determination to make his people real, he provides family background, wives, children, a few friends. However, the same flatness of characterization pervasive in most technothriller writing holds for these. Rarely do the families come alive. The wives and children are too perfect, friends too understanding, invariably good-humored and supportive. But the humanizing element in his characters (and a quality that adds to suspense) is that they can occasionally make mistakes. They misread, or overlook, or make a poor judgment that leads to serious consequences. Still, the effect of such action is seen to propel plot, not to alter or develop character. The military and government agents in the author's drama do not change with success or failure.

CONCLUSION

All the many facets of Clancy's work may explain the esteem in which
it is held by readers, and also the less praiseful attitudes of most literary
critics. While Clancy is an innovative and exciting writer in modern technological ways, paradoxically he is at the same time a traditional one. It
is not pejorative to call his work formula writing. The entertainment
technothriller, thriller, spy story always adheres to formula in language,
plot, images and symbols. We readers like the assurance of that familiarity, while at the same time we want something new added in character
or situation or "filler." (The filler is sometimes called "unbound motifs,"
that is, absorbing and interesting information but unnecessary to the pro-
gression of the story.) The pleasure readers gain from formula writing
is the repetition of something we have experienced and enjoyed before,
but with the excitement of newness. It might be the new plot or setting,
or more about the serial hero, of whom we know much, yet never
enough. We want to be told what he eats, drinks, drives, wears, what
he feels about the world in which he functions. And, with all that, in
such entertainments there is the promise of a complex world made comprehensible.

In Clancy's novels political views are central and powerful. He stirs
old and new fears of the Russian bear, the Red menace, creeping communism, Asians and Latins, all these personified through evil characters.
The enemy is known wherever or whenever he or she appears. The reader's apprehensions and the writer's become one. They are voiced by
Fleming Meeks, who tells us Clancy plays on our "deep-seated geopo-
litical fears" as he "spins scary scenarios of world chaos" (42). Works
become popular when the reader shares or sympathizes with the point
of view and feels a kinship to all or most of the values. Clancy brings
about most of these responses in readers, who cannot wait for each new
book to appear.

Then why the attacks of some reviewers on such popular material? To
answer that, we might consider a comment made by Kingsley Amis
about hostility to the James Bond novels of Ian Fleming. They, the critics,
are angered, says Amis, by the "attraction of something one disapproves
of" (x). But few readers disapprove. For most, the use of formula brings
the reassurance of safety even as the real or fictional world explodes.
Our various repressed needs and longings are served. Many of us have
an unconscious desire for danger and excitement, perhaps even violence,

though in reality most of us do everything to avoid involvement. Through thrillers/spy novels we can cross the boundaries of actual life into the world of the forbidden or unattainable. In our escape into the fantasized world we find wish fulfillment. We can confront our foes, knowing someone else will act for us and win. Our hero—ourself—will live to fight another day. Then, as the poet A. E. Housman tells us, we'll "see the world as the world's not" and ourselves as "sterling lad[s]" ("Terence, This Is Stupid Stuff").

The experience is cathartic. Whether we can finally decide that there is a single label for Clancy's work doesn't matter. Rather it is our understanding of the ways the pieces of the puzzle fit together to make up the world of Clancy's fiction.

NOTE

1. This is a line by Dilys Powell that Julian Symons quotes on p. 235 of *Mortal Consequences*.

3

The Hunt for Red October
(1984)

Clancy's friend Larry Bond, a designer of war games, was as surprised as everyone else at the success of Clancy's first novel. Adviser and collaborator on Clancy's second book (and later a novelist with his own collaborator), Bond failed to recognize the value of *The Hunt for Red October*. When he read the manuscript, he "just thought it was a good story, certainly not a blockbuster novel or the start of a whole new genre in fiction" (2). However, the novel did become a blockbuster, even though its publisher, the Naval Institute Press, was anything but a mainstream book company and had never before published a work of fiction nor had a best-selling book.

Although many reasons lie behind the immense popularity of the book, plot is undoubtedly the most important. It is more memorable than character, setting, or philosophic views. Simultaneously simple and complex, the story line appeals to a wide range of readers, those who enjoy thrillers or spy stories, science fiction, or military derring-do. A basic and familiar plot of hide and seek evolves into an intricate design when modern military technology is added.

PLOT DEVELOPMENT

The events of the novel occur prior to the breakup of the Soviet Union. According to Clancy, he was inspired partly by an actual event in 1975, when a Soviet destroyer, *Storozhevoy*, attempted to defect, not to America, but to Sweden. Through Clancy's fictional hero the true story of the defection is told to the fictional American president when the Central Intelligence Agency (CIA) informs him about unusual activities in the North Atlantic. That real mutiny failed. The fictional one will not, though of course nobody knows it as the story moves forward.

The action begins aboard a Soviet Typhoon–class nuclear submarine called the *Red October*, which is about to undertake a mission. Captain First Rank Marko Ramius, a man who is half-Russian and half-Lithuanian, is commander of the ship. Although Ramius is supposed to rendezvous in the Barents Sea for war games with the *V. K. Konovalov*, an Alpha-type nuclear submarine, the fastest and deepest-diving vessel in existence, Ramius has other plans. Instead of turning east, Ramius goes west-northwest. He intends to defect.

While his former commander and mentor heads out to sea from the Kola Fjord, Captain Second Rank Viktor Tupolev waits aboard the *Konovalov*. Soon he will be informed by his superiors of the treasonous action of Ramius, and his submarine with other ships of the Soviet fleet, surface and underwater, will be ordered to search for and destroy the *Red October*. Of all the naval commanders, Tupolev will come closest to fulfilling the mission, but even he will fail. In most spy/thrillers, and in all those written by Clancy, it is a given that the enemy must lose. In this plot the enemy is represented by Tupolev. For the Soviets it is vital that the *Red October* not fall into American hands, because the submarine has been built with a new drive system, one which exists only in Clancy's imagination. No other country possesses it, and that drive could give them underwater superiority. Nicknamed "the caterpillar," the drive system not only reduces cavitation sounds greatly, thus having the capacity to deceive and elude other ships, but it also operates on reduced power.

Before embarking on his journey, Ramius sent a letter announcing his intentions to Admiral Yuri Padorin, the chief political officer of the Soviet Navy. The inefficiency of the postal system in the Soviet Union causes a five-day delay before the letter arrives and action can be taken. By that time the USS *Dallas*, a 688-class submarine patrolling an area southwest of Iceland, has picked up foreign submarine sounds on its sonar equipment. Because the current mission of the *Dallas* is to watch and listen for vessels in the region known as "Red Route One," consisting of a series of underwater mountains of the Reykjanes Ridge, they are in position to hear the sounds coming from any submarines in the vicinity. When Sonarman Second Class Ronald Jones reports unusual noises to Captain Mancuso, commander of the *Dallas*, they realize something is amiss. An unexpected number of Russian submarines are in the area. Soon Mancuso and several other commanders will learn the reasons.

Meanwhile, Jack Ryan, a professor and former marine, now a civilian employed by the CIA, has flown from England to the United States with photos the British have taken of the new Soviet submarine, the *Red October*. At this point neither the British nor the Americans know about the unique Russian drive system, but they do know there is something peculiarly different about the appearance of the submarine. Ryan, with the permission of the CIA director, persuades an old Naval Academy friend, Skip Tyler, to interpret the films. As a result of Tyler's study, the CIA, the president, and the navy understand the reasons for the Soviet actions once they learn about Ramius's defection. And that knowledge has come from a Soviet spy.

"Cardinal," the code name for the Soviet spy inside the Kremlin, through a series of the most secret actions, has provided the CIA with information about sudden suspicious activities in Russia. (In Clancy's fourth novel, *The Cardinal of the Kremlin,* he will take center stage.) He has informed them of Ramius's letter, though not its details—a novelistic device important to the suspense element of the story. Upon receipt of the letter by Admiral Padorin large numbers of Soviet nuclear submarines and surface ships are sent out to locate and sink, if necessary, their own submarine, the *Red October*.

The American president decides that U.S. ships and planes will hunt for the *Red October* because of its prospective usefulness to American technology. Where the Russians undertake the hunt for reasons of destruction, the Americans want to take possession of the vessel secretly in order to study many of the parts: drive, missiles, reactor, and sonar. With input from multiple sources, particularly from Skip Tyler, plans are devised to capture the *Red October* and release its crew, deceiving them and the Soviets from first to last. With opposite intentions, the chase is on between the Soviets and the Americans, who are also helped by their allies, the British. In one action-laden scene after another, involving submarines, surface vessels, and planes, as well as political maneuvers, the story builds to a tense climax. Helped by American naval vessels, Ramius succeeds in eluding the Soviet pursuers, while at the same time destroying some of his enemies. The United States plan, that is, Skip Tyler's plan, works totally. Through the use of elaborate technology and political tactics, the Russians are duped into believing the *Red October* exploded and sank. But secretly the *Red October* is taken to Norfolk, Virginia, on the eighteenth day after Ramius leaves the Kola Fjord.

CHARACTERS

Supporting Characters

Although only Ryan and Ramius are the major players in the novel, a huge cast of lesser military figures has supporting roles. Because there are so many, they blend together, and it is sometimes difficult for the reader to keep track of them or their positions in the development of the story. On the American side there are admirals—rear admirals, vice admirals—military (and some civilian) directors of bureaus, captains, chiefs, commanders. Additionally, the American president has his staff of advisers, both military and civilian. Part of the difficulty of distinguishing the people is that they have few unique characteristics. Some are friendly, some unfriendly, some brusque, some courteous, some trusting, some suspicious, even of their own people. Some are merely ambitious, others, completely patriotic. A line or two describes most of them, and generally they are stock characters, "grade B" movie or television images.

The exceptions to these drab supporting players are three men, two of them, Mancuso and Jones, on the submarine the USS *Dallas*, and the third, Skip Tyler, at the Naval Academy. On the *Dallas*, Commander Bart Mancuso has the identifying marks as well as all the qualities of a Clancy hero, performing brilliantly and courageously from the moment he appears on the scene. Without Mancuso's daring, perseverance, intuitive qualities, and trust in his crew, the mission could not succeed. He takes seriously the reports of Sonarman Ronald Jones, an eccentric young electronic genius who is the first American seaman to recognize the sounds of the *Red October*. Both Mancuso and Jones are described in enough detail for the reader to have a continuing sense of their presence and personalities. Because the author has developed them as individuals, more than types, it comes as no surprise that both men appear in later Clancy novels. Another character who also shows up in other novels is Skip Tyler. Inasmuch as Tyler is of central importance in the American hunt for the Russian submarine, he too is accorded more description and dialogue than a number of other people.

The Soviet side has only a few decent, intelligent men in addition to

Ramius. Of these, the most memorable is Captain Lieutenant Grigoriy Kamarov. The navigator on the *Red October*, Kamarov is an outstanding seaman, the best and most trustworthy young sailor Ramius has known. He is like a son to Ramius, and he helps in the plan Ramius has devised to escape to freedom with the submarine. It is a bitter blow to the commander when Kamarov is killed in the final moments before the completion of their scheme, shot by a Soviet agent secreted aboard the *Red October*. Kamarov's death is paralleled by that of Captain Tupolev, who, like Kamarov, was also once a student of Ramius. But whereas Kamarov is totally loyal to Ramius, Tupolev, as a true Soviet man, has no qualms about attempting to kill his former teacher and destroy the *Red October*. Although it is ironic that both of Ramius's star pupils die, good does win out ultimately. Kamarov's death is not in vain, but Tupolev's is.

One other Soviet national stands out from the group, and that person, back in Russia, is Admiral Yuri Padorin. He had been Ramius's own mentor and patron. A great naval hero in World War II, Padorin barely survives his protégé's defection. However, his wiliness, learned over a lifetime of political maneuvering, preserves him. Clancy draws the old admiral as a complex man who is much more than his surface blandness might suggest. Padorin, unlike many of the other political figures, has an honorable history. He also has a questioning intelligence, which he is careful to hide, dignity, and courage. As a result, he seems unique among the oafish Soviet bureaucrats who merely shout, grunt, and threaten. Padorin succeeds in quietly outwitting them all.

Among the many characters in *Red October* none of the active players is female. Various reviewers have commented about the scarcity of women in Clancy's work. When he offers a terse explanation, it is not very satisfactory. He appears to be uncomfortable portraying women. In 1988, after he'd produced several novels, Clancy was the guest speaker at an FBI Academy seminar in Quantico, Virginia, where he reacted coolly to a question about the dearth of women in his work: "I've never been a woman, so I don't know much about the woman's point of view" (Friend 271). Given the fact that some of the greatest women characters in literature were created by male novelists, Clancy's answer seems limited, at best. Again in 1993 Clancy gave precisely the same reply to the same question of a call-in viewer on a talk show.

Clancy's first novel establishes the minor role that women play in most of his work. The two women we hear about in *Red October* but never encounter are Natalya, the late wife of Captain Ramius, and Caroline, wife of Jack Ryan.

Only the most superficial details are given about either woman. Natalya's importance to Marko, as well as to the mechanics of plot, provides
the impetus for her husband's defection. Through Ramius's bitter
thoughts about her unnecessary death we learn of their childlessness. He
leaves no family behind in the Soviet Union, a central issue for those
thinking of leaving the Rodina (homeland). He also muses about her
mothering of the young seamen under his command. Everyone admired
her, even those that Ramius considers political enemies. But kind, loving,
self-effacing Natalya died as a result of the incompetent and corrupt
Soviet medical system. The reader has no consciousness of Natalya as
an actual person. Instead, she seems a flat outline of a rather saintly
victim of the Communist hierarchal way of life. Through such bloodless
characters as Natalya, Clancy composes his pictures at an exhibition, that
is, life in the Soviet Union.

Dr. Caroline (Cathy) Ryan has even less of a function than Mrs. Ramius in *Red October*, even though she is alive and well in Marlow, an area
in the outskirts of London where her husband works. The reader never
sees her, but in a few scattered lines we are told about her. An ophthal-
mological surgeon, she serves as an instructor on an exchange program
at a hospital in London. Also, she plays the piano. Aside from those
details we know little about her life in England. Caroline Ryan is more
of a shadowy presence than Mrs. Ramius. She seems to be in the book
only to establish the picture of Ryan as a family man devoted to his wife
and two children. However, there is no information about their life together and almost none about her as an individual. When Jack Ryan flies
off to America to report to his superiors shortly before Christmas, his
one family concern (adding a jarringly sentimental and out-of-place note)
is to find a Skiing Barbie doll for his little girl, Sally. As Clancy continues
to develop the character and importance of Jack Ryan in succeeding
books, he gives Cathy Ryan more lines and activities. She has an important role in the first book the novelist wrote, but published third,
Patriot Games. Cathy Ryan is an unknown in *The Hunt for Red October*,
where she serves only as an appendage to her husband.

The Two Heroes

Although Ryan and Ramius are the two central figures in the novel,
Ramius is present from the very first page, whereas Ryan appears somewhat later and with little fanfare. Nothing alerts us to his importance.

Perhaps that accounts for the fact that the Russian commander catches and holds the attention of the reader more than Ryan does. Of the two, Ramius is the more exciting and engrossing man. The powerful action-filled introduction to Ramius makes Ryan appear lackluster when he comes on the scene. Ramius is shown in bitter Arctic weather, aboard his missile submarine in an ice-laden channel, as he prepares for departure to sea. Ryan is seen at his computer.

Clancy has said that he hadn't planned to use Ryan in this novel until he realized there was need for someone who would provide a type of narrative cohesiveness. Because he had begun work years earlier on what was to become *Patriot Games*, he decided that his major character in that unpublished novel could fill the required role in *Red October*. And, in fact, the author connects the two books by telling of an incident that occurs in an earlier period in *Patriot Games*. Ryan was given an honorary knighthood, the result of his having foiled terrorists intent on assassinating two people in Britain. These people, we later discover in *Patriot Games*, are members of the British royal family. Because it is essential to the plot of that novel, Clancy develops the episodes fully. But in *Red October* it is only an incident linked to Ryan's going to work for the CIA as a member of a British and American liaison group.

Ryan is a laid-back character who, when tested, proves to have all the right stuff. Among his numerous qualifications for his present job is his earlier service as a marine. However, there is one problem attached to his work. As a result of his experiences in the marines when he was seriously injured in a plane crash, he prefers not to fly and is very jittery aboard planes (much like Clancy himself). But when ordered on a mission that involves hazardous flights, he does his duty. Even if it means braving a dangerously heavy wind aboard an aircraft carrier to do something he dislikes almost as much as flying, which is climbing a ladder into a plane, he executes it with good humor. The pilot of that plane, a Harrier, tests Ryan's mettle, but they gain mutual respect for each other almost immediately. This lays the groundwork for a characteristic response to Ryan in book after book. If at first men are not impressed by him, they soon have reason to reverse their initial judgment.

By the end of *Red October* Ryan has lost his fear of flying (temporarily, anyhow) and is relaxed enough to sleep aboard a plane that is returning him to London. We learn about him from this and similar episodes. He never turns away from danger but meets all challenges as they arrive. And always he gains increased respect from the people around him.

Such types of situations are paradigmatic for Ryan. He may be nervous about meeting the president and making a presentation before him, but he does his job so superbly that he impresses the president as well as everyone else he meets. Failure is outside his experience. Thus, when given a dual task by the president, to provide information to American commanders about the *Red October* and to bring back information about the British (something Ryan regards uncomfortably as spying), he accepts the task even though he would prefer otherwise. Nevertheless, he never regards himself as a spy and states that emphatically when asked the question later by a Russian naval officer. Still, as expected by his superiors, he performs magnificently. Resolute and brave, he also becomes involved in physical actions, helping to save both the *Red October* and its commander.

This hero has every remarkable quality except outstanding looks. Unlike the eyecatching appearance of other thriller superheroes such as James Bond, Ryan's is rather ordinary. Although it is improbable that Clancy would deliberately have chosen Bond as a model for his hero, the English spy inevitably comes to mind. Bond is one of the forerunners of thriller heroes and an important even if unconscious influence on the work of successive generations of thriller writers. The reader also thinks of Bond because his adversaries were also almost invariably Soviet and because both he and Ryan have been called flat characters by literary critics. Just as the term "cardboard booby" has stuck to Bond, so too has the label of dull cardboard character stuck to Ryan. A difference, however, is that Bond has an image of glamour and glitter, whereas nothing suggests romance or mystery about Ryan. Who could imagine Bond sitting in front of a television set at all? Ryan, though, is described as watching a three-hour football game. His American qualities are seen through such interests, although the author might be attempting to glamorize (and Anglicize?) Ryan when he speaks of grouse shooting with a member of the aristocracy in Scotland. This is more Bondian than Ryanesque. It doesn't work and instead adds a false note.

Ryan's waist is thickening because he often neglects exercise (a point that apparently appeals to Clancy inasmuch as he describes Mancuso, as well as a character in his next book, *Red Storm Rising*, as having that problem also). However, Ryan is a perfectly acceptable size 42 long. Although expensive, his suits from England's exclusive Savile Row are neither unusual nor mod. Ryan's blue eyes are neither sparkling nor piercing but instead have a vacant look. That is deceptive, the omniscient author tells us, for Ryan is a man whose thoughts frequently are turned to research. In his rational and intellectual abilities he surpasses almost everyone. The military needs more men like him, we are informed on several occasions by various people. Every operation, from one novel to the next, seems to be on the verge of foundering unless Ryan takes charge.

Completely open, Ryan does not practice subterfuge. When he doesn't know the answer to a question, he says so. The most attractive quality about Ryan, in this book, is his modesty. (That changes as the series develops.) Hero he may be, but Clancy tries to make him human by noting that, like the rest of us, Ryan doesn't always follow explanations of complex activities. He understands "about half" of what the British describe of their submarine actions. And when telling Ramius that he is not a naval officer but an analyst for "the Dark Force," the CIA, he says, "this is one Dark Force who's probably going to wet his pants before we're finished here" (217).

Although unpretentious in his view of self, Ryan is fabulously rich. That is a reminder of the influence of the British detective stories of the Golden Age. The 1920s and 1930s sleuths were usually independently wealthy, and several of them had titles as well; recall again Lord Peter Wimsey. Because of Ryan's fortune, at the time he appears in the novel he has no interest in making money. Four years as a stockbroker provided all he would need. His superior at the CIA speculates that Ryan got bored with those activities. Also learned, he has a Ph.D. in economics and history, is successful in everything, and is happily married. Ryan seems to have led a charmed life. The reader knows he has a bright future as well.

In spite of, perhaps because of all his stellar qualities, Ryan is a surprisingly uninteresting figure. There is nothing questioning nor rebellious in him. His world has meaning. It has no existential philosophers such as Jean-Paul Sartre or Albert Camus, whom he abhors. No psychologists either. He considers them ignorant. The flatness of Ryan as a character may be accounted for in his lack of introspection, a deficiency in a man of his education. One might argue that is a major reason that we prefer Ramius. He is a man of multiple layers. Perhaps the Soviet system is responsible for that kind of complexity. A man as open as Ryan could not survive, but Ramius has.

Whenever Ramius appears on the scene, the episode is charged with vitality. We learn of his emotions and the reasons behind them. His motives for defection are examined, although some reviewers find them insufficient for his drastic actions. Ramius is a man who has suffered deeply in every sense. He never knew his Russian mother, who died in childbirth, and his Lithuanian father left the boy's upbringing to his own mother, a religious woman who imbued in her grandson knowledge of right and wrong. Religious practices were forbidden in the Communist sphere. As a result of such harsh rules, the old woman, like other believers, had to be careful. Nevertheless, she had the infant Marko baptized. The moral lessons, though not the dogma of religion, remain a part of his character. He has come to believe that Marxism has "cast aside the objective measure of justice and ethics which . . . was the principal legacy of religion to civilized life" (25).

Because of the brutality of Stalinists such as his father toward his own countrymen, the child was caught in a dual existence. Although his father held a very high position, Marko had almost no friends. The elder Ramius's career was built on loyalty to the Communist party. Furthermore, he was a hero of the Battle of Leningrad. Unfortunately, he was also a political fanatic, a member of Lenin's Red Guards. It was Aleksandr Ramius who saw to it that those Lithuanians who were disloyal to the Marxist-Leninist state were put to death. In his early childhood, Marko loved and admired his father. Knowing his father to be a hero and a kind parent, he was proud to be the son of a party chief. But as he grew up, he began to understand that much of what he was being taught disturbed his sense of justice, of humanity, of right and wrong. He could not avoid associating his father with the society that more and more he came to dislike.

To survive in the culture in which he lived, young Ramius paid lip service to a creed in which he did not believe. Although he joined the important youth organizations and participated in their activities, early in life he became a questioner. Of course, it had to be inward. The system allowed no deviations. When he was eight, his solitariness led him to friendship with an old, politically disgraced sea captain who showed him a different world, the freedom of life on the sea, and in a short time sowed the seeds for Marko's future. The young Ramius knew early that he wanted to be a naval officer. He was only in his teens when he chose submarines for his special interest, this at a time that they were extremely primitive vessels. Nevertheless, it was clear to him that underwater ships were the vanguard of future naval warfare. His brilliance in school, with honors in everything, brought him to the attention of various naval commanders, and his father's position made it possible for him to advance rapidly. However, most of his achievements resulted from merit. Through hands-on experience and training, Ramius became a nuclear expert and commander in the submarine fleet.

Chosen always to test every new class of submarine, Marko was recognized as an extraordinary seaman. Not only did he know everything about submarines, but he was also a much admired and respected leader. He looked after his men, the good and the bad. Nevertheless, he never achieved the rank of admiral because he did not play the Communist game of politics. His concessions to the system were to join the Party and to keep silent about the corruptness of the system. Only the death of his wife could alter that.

The Americans know Ramius as a "hotshot." What they don't know about is his cool head in all circumstances and his long cultivated quality of careful planning. Both attributes are central in the successful conclusion of his actions. Though wounded, Ramius, with considerable help from the United States, and from Ryan in particular, saves the *Red October* and brings it into Norfolk.

Whether or not Clancy intended it, Ryan and Ramius appear to be both foils—contrasts—and doubles—much alike in certain ways to each other. (A convention in literature suggests that type of doubling when the author gives the same initial or initials to two characters.) There are a number of similarities as well as many differences in the men. Ramius seems fearless, whereas Ryan, though also courageous, shows some apprehension before plunging into difficult situations. But then, Ryan has a family and a life he believes in, whereas Ramius has little to lose, having been deprived of the human part of his existence. Ramius has an established reputation. Ryan still has his to build, although everyone makes it clear he could rest on his many earlier successes. Ryan is totally loyal to his country, unlike Ramius, but would Ryan be so in a country as corrupt as the Soviet Union that Clancy depicts?

Although Ryan has had several career changes, Ramius, a single-minded man insofar as profession is concerned, has spent his entire life becoming a great submariner. Thus, Ramius's sacrifice strikes us as extraordinary, daring and admirable beyond measure. It also takes a type of hardness. Ramius is more indurate than Ryan, able to commit acts we cannot imagine Ryan capable of at this point in fictional time. Clearly, both men are brilliant in everything they undertake, yet total opposites in training and orientation. Clancy has drawn each man to represent what is best about his country: bravery, strength, dedication, morality. Still, the author does not intend Ramius to be a typical Soviet citizen, for his strong moral nature is closer to what Clancy sees as American. Ryan, in spite of his vast accomplishments which are surely not characteristic of all Americans, is a representative all-American hero.

STYLE

Clancy's techniques in this novel are characteristic of successive work. There is humor, both in Ryan's dialogue and in the author's comments. Some of the language—though not enough—is varied to fit character and personalities. Conversations are limited, so that the reader is conscious of the author's voice. Technology is paramount, and the acronyms are often baffling. Still, suspense builds from beginning to end.

Part of Ryan's charm is his sense of humor. Ryan has a dry wit, which is also true of his creator. The voice of the author interjects occasional verbal jabs similar to Ryan's. The author: "One of the compensations for wearing a uniform and earning less money than an equally talented man can make in the real world is the off chance of being killed" (256). Ryan, telling Ramius about himself, speaks of the books he has written about naval history, including one about Admiral William F. ("Bull") Halsey. When Ramius, who has read the book, disagrees with Ryan's viewpoint, Ryan responds: "You will do well in my country, Captain Ramius. You are already a book critic" (283). The reader wishes there would be more of that kind of humor, because it adds a needed dimension to Ryan's personality.

Ryan's language is more subtle than that of the career military men. In numerous parts of the novel Clancy describes in salty language the thoughts he attributes to military men. An old admiral who has come up through the ranks believes "the CIA had too many men whose only skill was kissing ass" (45). And, in one of the infrequent lines of dialogue, a quartermaster announces to his bunkmate: "The old man knows his shit" (205). Clancy sprinkles in the vulgarity and colloquialisms that are part of the military world. Once in a while he will be ungrammatical in an attempt toward verisimilitude, as when an assistant to the director of naval intelligence is heard to say, "Him and Saunders over at Sea Systems" (43). Unlike most contemporary thriller writers, Clancy does not spice up this early work with sex. There is scarcely anything that might be considered a sexual remark. Overt sexual language or sexual scenes are simply not part of the text, although the language is clearly masculine. When he talks of Skip Tyler's "zest for life," he follows it up with a statement about the number of children the Tylers have, but *Red October* contains neither descriptions nor discussion of sexual encounters. That will change with the third novel.

This story has a minimal amount of dialogue. Only as the action and suspense become taut is more direct language used. When East meets West aboard the *Red October* and the Soviet and American seamen and officers come face-to-face, the author briefly stands aside, allowing them to speak. However, the words frequently sound labored. No doubt Clancy means to capture the differences in speech and culture, but he is no more effective here than in many other conversations. We expect language to reveal personality and even character, yet the spoken lines often are so indistinguishable from each other that they could be transferred from one person to another. Dialogue is just not Clancy's strong suit. Most of the time we are listening to the voice of the author describing people, their thoughts, and events past and present. His is a technique that is more "tell" than "show" in this novel.

That authorial voice, however, is one which readers find engrossing, even when we disagree with his statements. His presence comes through in point of view, politics, and philosophy. It keeps us turning pages regardless of our own position. The variations of the authorial sound, the shifts in rhythm pique and excite us. At the end of many scenes we can almost hear the change of tone. The voice drops with the short final sentence—a few conclusive words: "He knew it was tapped" (57); "He was becoming a weapon" (67); "Ryan was sure he wouldn't, and he was right" (97); "Four pairs of eyes blinked in unison" (256). Having caught and held us, the author then shifts to a completely different setting and situation.

By far the most potent elements of Clancy's style are his mastery of technology and his ability to maintain suspense throughout his long novels. Not surprisingly, his use of technology is what reviewers write of, readers talk about, and military experts praise. It has been reported frequently that his expertise in technology and his ability to weave a novel around that in this first book and successive ones account for the author's continuing popularity. Nevertheless, not everyone appreciates the emphasis on the technological elements. Some reviewers claim the technology is like a character in the book, perhaps the most important one. Among them are those who think the technological parts are overdone, that less detail about submarines and submarine warfare would have made a better book.[1]

Reviewers also point to the difficulty with acronyms, of which there are enough to have led to the publication of *The Tom Clancy Companion*, a concordance not only to *The Hunt for Red October* but later novels up through *The Sum of All Fears*. Generally Clancy tells us in advance what the many initials represent, but he doesn't always do so. Sometimes he

uses the acronym before explaining the full term. Occasionally the definition of the acronyms is delayed so that we only understand them
through the discussion of the event. A reviewer for the *Wall Street Journal*
calls the acronyms "mysterious" and writes that he "sometimes had no
idea what weapons were being pointed or what kind of equipment was
being discussed until contextual clues made things clear" (Alden 28). Of
course, there is always the problem for nonmilitary people of remembering later what the definition was, given the large number of acronyms. In a single line, Ryan, reminding a vice admiral of all the agencies
that came into being after Pearl Harbor, lists "the CIA, DIA, NSA, and
NRO, among others" (71).

In spite of the challenge of the technology and the acronyms, the
reader is hooked by the suspense of *The Hunt for Red October*. Clancy
employs multiple strategies to maintain suspense. His introductory chapter here, as well as in successive books, is powerful, and one might argue
that it is the strongest chapter in the novel. As is not the case in some
of the later chapters, not a word is wasted in that opening. Clancy explains nothing here. Painting the scene without embellishment, he
quickly pulls the reader into the story through the force of the prose.
The first paragraph is a description of the Russian protagonist, Ramius,
the intensely cold weather, the harbor, the dock that has held the submarine, and the "stolid" appearance of the Russian workers who watch
the submarine move out of the fjord. By the end of the beginning section,
"The First Day," a chapter of only a few pages, the suspense is so strong
that the reader eagerly moves on, propelled partly by the shortness of
the chapters. The fast pace is sustained by a series of subsections within
the chapter, usually three or four, different from the previous and following section. Thus, a chapter may have a segment set in the office of
Admiral Padorin in Moscow, then a section aboard the USS *Dallas*, and
a third at CIA headquarters. The brevity of each part within a chapter
increases the sense of rapid movement. Time seems to be hurrying along,
as if a clock is ticking and mimicking the sensation of a chase. Although
the events that take place at sea are naturally the most tense and exciting,
other episodes take on the elements of haste and stress because of the
rapidity of movement and frequent change of locale.

Another element of suspense comes from the withholding of vital bits
of information. That tried and true technique is essential to detective
stories, but is not always part of spy/thriller fiction. When a writer does
utilize it, he increases the emotions even more. With a Turn-of-the-Screw
methodology, the novelist tightens the tension of the plot. Throughout
Red October Clancy provides partial information. In characteristic use of

the technique, he hints and holds back. This, combined with the rapid shifts of scene and episode, greatly heightens the suspense. An example of this combination may be seen in the episodes which involve the letter Ramius sends to Admiral Padorin. We are informed of it early, but it takes five days for Padorin to receive the letter. Then there is some delay in his reading of it, and when we do witness his response, we still do not know what the letter says.

THEMATIC ISSUES

In its clear political stance *Red October* is similar to most, though not all spy or political thrillers. The enemy is clear and identifiable. "We" (Americans) are better than "they" (foreigners, Soviets) are. The outcome of any struggle between us is predictable. America will win, no matter what. The philosophy is manichean: good versus evil. We are the good, they the bad. Russians murder anyone if it is politically expedient, even in peacetime. Americans do not, even when the people are the enemy. In this rather simple worldview everything "we" do is superior. Unfortunately, America must constantly defend itself and the world against the monsters wherever they are, or we and the world will come to grief. Eternal vigilance is required, a theme Clancy repeats in book after book, not only in his novels but in his nonfiction work as well.

Clancy reveals his views openly, but with some dissembling. Although he insists his primary interest is entertainment, his pronouncements do not read that way. In interviews his focus is on military matters, weaponry, and conservative political philosophy. In *Red October* the same themes are sounded. Most of his praise is given to the navy, but he finds fault with the CIA, and various parts of the military establishment which needs more heroes. As the story unfolds, his strongest criticism is reserved for the U.S. Congress, which, he suggests, cannot be trusted to maintain secrecy or to make the "right" decisions. The novelist's "real"-life anti-Congress theme is established in this novel, and successive works continue it.

ALTERNATE READING: THE NOVEL AS
GENERIC FORMULA

Although various theoretical readings may be applied to novels, one particular type that works well for most detective, spy, thriller fiction is that of formulaic structuralism.[2] All fiction has structure, but the thriller novel follows a formula in its structure. To read a novel in this manner, we analyze the methods and style the writer uses to fit his work into a particular formula. However, the reader imposes the requirements more than the writer, since the novelist is directing the work to a particular audience. The suspense mode of fiction calls for simple syntax, much detail, and significant action.

Language chosen by the author fits within agreed-upon conventions that are understood by the reader, but language also influences the reader's attitudes and interpretations. The form (how the story is told) usually matters more than content (what is told), though in Clancy's case it is often more content than form. The pieces of a plot or plots must fit together like a puzzle, and the relationship of all parts must be preserved. When those pieces are all in place, the plot is resolved. With Clancy's work, no matter how many subplots he may introduce, at the end every plot fits. Although a plot in a thriller novel may appear to be new and fresh, in its basic outline it is really a variation on the other plots. Appeal then comes through the variations. When stripped down, Clancy's plots are familiar, but the technology makes the novels unique.

In formulaic fiction characters are less important than the events, because the characters are generic, unreal, and molded as exigencies arise. Depth of character or changes in character are rare in such novels. Thus it is surprising to read reviews which criticize Clancy's characters excessively. These reviewers are indifferent or hostile to a generic formula and because of that are annoyed by what they consider Clancy's indifference to character. Most of them claim he is more interested in gadgets or hardware than in people. That would place Clancy's work in the same category as Ian Fleming's Bond books and films. Yet, fairly or unfairly, critics seem to demand more of Clancy.

Behind all events, the formulaic structure's received system of rules leads to a predetermined outcome. There is a code that carries over from text to text. The reader of *Red October* knows from the outset that Americans and those who side with them will defeat the Soviets. Rules governing the text preordain that. Good men are rewarded, and bad men meet some type of anticipated justice. (These rewards and punishment are only for men, since women have no role in *Red October*.) Because Clancy's fictional world is not complex, even if the technology is, the system works. The parts fall into place, and a fictional history is created.

A generic reading of thrillers requires certain cause-and-effect development. Something sets an action in place. In *Red October* it is the action taken by the commander of the Soviet submarine *Red October*. A type of order that has existed in each country is disturbed. For both countries the goal is a different resolution of the problem. Complications arise from the initial episode, which brings about the involvement of the heroic protagonist. In this novel the author's choice of hero is Jack Ryan. Ramius may seem equally impressive or more so than Ryan, but that is not likely to be the author's intent.

Ryan, like almost all thriller heroes, is a superior human being. The reader recognizes his role almost immediately because of his inherent resemblance to other heroes. In accordance with the structural formula, he is challenged again and again and performs worthy deeds. Although at first glance it may not seem that he is being put into testing situations, eventually that becomes clear. He is measured several times by varying circumstances and passes every test. It devolves on him to restore order. He is not alone in his mission. Many brave men join in what is considered a worthy cause, to save the Russian sub and its crew, to deceive the Soviets, and to gain useful knowledge. Justice in the form of battles and daring deeds assures that the good side will be victorious. Here multiple units of the U.S. military serve that function. Battle is done, the final pieces come together, and order is restored.

The success of the novel depends in great measure on the formulaic structure. In *Red October* the narrator tells the story to a special, almost preselected audience which understands the message of the work. They and the author share and understand an agreed-on code. If the code is followed, as it is here, the expectations and desires of the audience are fulfilled.

NOTES

1. For comments about the importance of technology over character and also criticism of the overload of technical material, see the reviews of John Sherman in *West Coast Review of Books*, November-December 1984: 30; and Richard Setlowe in *Los Angeles Times Book Review*, 9 Dec. 1984: 2.

2. Structuralism is defined in many ways. Here I am following Tzvetan Todorov's *The Fantastic* (1973). In his view of mystery fiction, structure is an essential ingredient.

Red Storm Rising
(1986)

Tom Clancy's second book has only his name on the cover and title page. Information on the jacket is also limited to Clancy. No mention is made of a second author; yet the novel is the work of two people, Clancy and his friend Larry Bond who once served as a naval surface warfare officer. In the Author's Note Clancy writes but does not explain why "Larry's name does not appear on the title page [but] this book is as much his as mine. We never did figure out the division of labor." Both men shared the royalty money. Presumably, then, the attribution to Clancy alone as author has to do with the enormous success of *Red October* and his name recognition for the book-buying public. (Bond obviously learned that this was a useful tactic. When his own novel, *Red Phoenix*, was published in 1989, only the name of Larry Bond appeared on the cover and title page. The reader has to look very closely at the introductory material to discover that it too was a collaborative effort, this time between Bond and another person named Patrick Larkin. By 1989 Bond had achieved his own name recognition.)

Although *Red Storm Rising* is considered Clancy's, the novel has all the signs of Bond's martial knowledge. Bond, a designer of war games, had influenced the choice of material for Clancy's earlier work, and for the second novel the two men decided to coauthor a book structured on the model of war games in Europe and the North Atlantic region. Information from Bond's commercial game Harpoon had been extremely useful to Clancy in *Red October*. Harpoon and a newer game, Convoy, had a part in the planning of *Red Storm Rising*.

Many nonmilitary people know war games only as entertainment, and they buy that kind of program for their home computers. Tom Clancy, who had no experience or professional ties to the military, played war games before and after becoming a writer. In the same way that his friendship with Larry Bond resulted from Clancy's interest in the military games Bond had designed, his technological novels led to a close relationship with military people. After publication and the resulting popularity of the first two Clancy books, the novels became available as games in computer stores.

In fact, war games are more than computer toys. They exist in another form, which is used by the military services to develop the strategies and tactical warfare skills of personnel. Scenarios of the games generally are based on the latest political and military intelligence of potential enemies and their ability to take offensive action against the United States and its allies. War games serve as preparation for counteroffensive actions in What If? situations. In such games, computers are a basic tool of training exercises for actual troops and equipment that test theoretical situations. The games hone the skills of military personnel in every phase of warfare, preparing them for actual combat.

PLOT DEVELOPMENT

Red Storm Rising is a futuristic story involving large areas of the globe. Although no date is given, the time does not seem very distant from the present, because there are few political changes in the future world that is depicted. Ironically, those momentous events that have altered the balance of power, names, and borders of countries since this book was written have not yet occurred. Europe in the novel still has its old boundaries. The Soviet Union continues as a single united country. These and other major "facts" of the novel are now anachronisms, that is, a wrong time reference; but when the book was published in 1986, the powerful Soviet Union had not been dissolved nor its threats turned hollow. In the United States all the familiar agencies and divisions of government remain in place. The North Atlantic Treaty organization (NATO) serves as a deterrent force in the Western world. The pettiness, competition, and jealousies within the bureaucracies of individual countries and the distrust between world powers remain as strong as ever in the futuristic world. These animosities trigger a third world war when a catastrophic event takes place in the Soviet Union.

In Siberia a group of Muslim terrorists blow up the most important oil refinery in the Soviet Union. These Azerbaijanis want vengeance on the "godless" Russians who have patronized and humiliated them, but the effect of their action is felt around the world. When presented with the estimate of damage to their economy, members of the Politburo decide they will remedy their loss by seizing the oil fields of the Persian Gulf. Without oil, much of the industry in the Soviet Union would shut down, and the daily needs of ordinary people could not be met. Because the Russians think in terms of strength and control, they do not want other countries to know about the oil shortages they face. Political paranoia convinces them that knowledge of their weakness would play into the hands of their adversaries.

Human limitations serve the side of the Soviets. Although the United States learns about the explosions in Siberia through information conveyed by satellites, nothing much is deduced from it. When notice of the event is provided to various military stations, in addition to the CIA and French and British allies, nobody anticipates what is to happen. In a short time the event fades into memory. Even after war breaks out, the Western countries do not link the hostilities with the oil disaster in Siberia. The Soviets attack on land, sea, and in the air, surprising all the countries involved; but not until the hostilities are almost over do the opposing forces learn from a captured Russian flier about the shortage of oil in his country. This quickly leads to a change of allied tactics and the collapse of the Soviet forces.

Almost every segment of the tightly constructed plot centers around military planning and combat once the war begins. Prior to the initial Soviet attacks, a few aggressive members of the Politburo secretly devise a scheme reminiscent of the subterfuge of Adolf Hitler when he usurped control in Germany in the 1930s. They arrange a bombing attack on the Kremlin, knowing that a number of Russian children will be visiting there at the time. The children die, and the public is aroused by the propaganda that follows. When the Soviet government declares that the culprits are West German, World War III begins. Soviet troops invade Germany. At the same time a surprise attack is launched on a strategic air base in Iceland, achieving an early important victory for control of the North Atlantic region. According to Clancy, "Iceland is the key to

Europe. If we hold Iceland, the Russian job of closing the North Atlantic goes from difficult to damn near impossible. That's why, in *Red Storm Rising*, we let the Soviets neutralize Iceland" (Cooper 62).

The mission in the Soviet attack at sea is the destruction of surface and underwater vessels in order to prevent counterattacks and the delivery of supplies by convoy from the United States. These efforts are needed for the Soviet objective, which is the subjugation of forces that could prevent them from obtaining the oil they need and want. Each side fights with everything it has, except nuclear power and chemical gases. Neither the Russians nor the Americans choose to take the chance of unleashing those deadly forces, yet the fear of such attacks persists. When Clancy was questioned about his decision to omit the use of nuclear force in a novel about a third world war, he credited the Russians with knowing that certain limits must be set in warfare, if only in self-interest. Discussion in the novel about the possible use of nuclear weapons and also of chemical gases makes it clear that both kinds of destructive elements must be avoided. Chemical gases are to be feared even more than nuclear attack, declares the commander in chief of the German Republic Democratic Forces (East Germany), another anachronism, since Germany was reunified in October 1990. The German general states, "It is actually easier to protect our citizens from nuclear weapons than against gases" (131).

The war wreaks terrible damage in Europe, but neither the United States nor the Soviet Union is attacked. Here Clancy departs from the historic pattern of earlier wars in which Russia was invaded by hostile forces. Except for the lack of nuclear weapons and chemical gas, the future war is total. Submarines "kill" other submarines as well as surface vessels. Reconnaissance planes locate targets, and other planes drop missiles on them, bombing ships and bases and shooting down enemy planes. Armies fight to gain or preserve territory—the Russians to advance westward, the German and NATO troops to contain the enemy and prevent him from moving forward. All the battles are brutal, no matter where they take place.

Weapons familiar and unfamiliar to the reader are used. For a period of time, in one suspenseful engagement after another, it seems as if the Soviets cannot be defeated, but the war goes on longer than anticipated, and the same reason that has led to the war brings about its end: the Russian shortage of oil. When the Allies attack the oil reinforcements the Russian have brought to the German front, the choice for the Russian invader is annihilation of their own troops or surrender. A brave Russian general sees the inevitable conclusion and, wanting to save the remnant of his and other Soviet forces, negotiates the surrender. After a brilliantly planned and executed coup purges the Politburo of its corrupt leader and his followers, negotiations result, and peace returns to the western world.

CHARACTERS

Once again, Clancy has filled the canvas with a vast number of people, and again most of the military figures are male, except for a lone female pilot. The remaining players are those who have served in government or the military. The handful of women include the pilot, a single Icelandic woman, and the wives of men attached to some branch of service. As in *Red October*, Americans and friendly colleagues outnumber Soviet characters, so that the reader remembers the Russians more easily than the majority of the Allies. In addition to the Americans, military personnel and administrators from various other NATO countries fill out the cast. Some of the people are named and developed briefly, but the rest are merely part of the background troops. While the reader may struggle to scan the huge stage filled with characters performing very different tasks, Clancy captures the authenticity of war as he constantly shifts from one battle scene to another. As in a replication of an actual war, the struggle takes precedence over people. Throughout the centuries, men, no matter how courageous, have been faceless parts of the group, ours or theirs. Few are singled out for fame or even for recognition amongst those who fight and are victorious. Far more fight and fall "unknelled, uncoffined, and unknown" (George Gordon Lord Byron, *Childe Harold* canto IV, line 1611). In the novel, brief homage is paid to those unnamed men by their commanders who can do little more in the midst of battle. Grief and anguish must be postponed.

Heroes fight and die on both sides of the Iron Curtain, but Clancy personalizes a number of Americans in contrast to a smaller group of the Soviet stalwarts. These men courageously defy the dictatorship of the single-minded corrupt leaders. Different from the limited number of astute, judicious Soviet men, all the Americans are independent and intelligent, although brave men from every country are willing to sacrifice their lives. No character functions throughout the novel as a narrative or cohesive center in the way Jack Ryan did in the first book. Ryan, a major player in most Clancy novels, does not appear in *Red Storm Rising*.

Instead the author utilizes representative figures from a few areas of the American military spectrum. Usually they appear in separate segments and actions throughout the story. And while this technique succeeds in maintaining swift pacing and suspense, it works against the development of reader interest in characters.

Three of the four people whose actions are traced in different parts of the novel are in the navy, and the fourth is in the air force. They are Commander Daniel McCafferty, of the submarine *Chicago* (an actual 688-class submarine); Robert Toland, a navy reservist and analyst for the National Security Agency, "recruited" by the navy when needed and stationed aboard the nuclear aircraft carrier *Nimitz* (also a famous ship); Ed Morris, commander of the USS *Pharris,* a 1052-class frigate (serving in the U.S. Navy since 1974), whose task in this war is to escort convoys across the Atlantic. McCafferty is the admirable type of military figure Clancy portrays in novel after novel. A strong leader, he is liked and respected by his men. Toland shows the importance of intelligence analysis. But it is also through him that the author shows it is possible to underestimate a man's ability. Ed Morris represents the heroic military people who put personal feelings aside when necessary. Morris feels guilty when his ship is torpedoed and a large number of the crew are lost, but he knows that duty requires him to return to battle and help achieve victory.

Then there is the man on whom many of the events of the story focus, Air Force First Lieutenant Mike Edwards, a meteorologist stationed in Keflavik, Iceland. Although each of the four has a crucial role in the winning of the war, and each has the qualifications for a hero, Edwards is the man we learn most about. He is the author's choice to fill the archetypal role of knight-at-arms.

A Mythical Hero

At first Edwards seems a most unlikely candidate for the role of hero. His military training has not prepared him for the events that single him out. He has been with his squadron only two months when the war begins. He and three enlisted marines are the only survivors of a Russian bombing of the airport base at Keflavik. No other Americans are left there at the ruined base or elsewhere in Iceland. Although he lacks experience, in the tradition of all services Edwards as the only officer must become the leader for his little group until they are rescued. Their survival depends on his ability to make the right decisions and choices in a country overrun by the Russian invaders. The men have to find the means to stay alive in the harsh northern climate and terrain, with no shelter, little food, and constant watchfulness to avoid the enemy forces.

When Edwards is first introduced in chapter 18, almost 200 pages into the story, he appears to be nothing more than another character in another dangerous place. A pleasant, unprepossessing young man, Edwards initially shows none of the visible marks of a traditional hero. Though he is well aware of the strategic importance of the base, his own job nevertheless seems unimportant, even trivial to him, part of the meaningless work and plans often inherent to military service. But he accepts his role with humor then and later. Not long before he gets involved with life-threatening and life-saving actions, he thinks about the insignificance of his job in wartime as a meteorologist: "As if someone might need an especially deadly weather chart with which to attack an incoming bomber!" (177).

His sense of superfluity disappears as soon as he becomes responsible for other men. Edwards's transformation jogs the reader's memory into a comparison to the twentieth-century prototypical knight, the mild-mannered Clark Kent, whose appearance and personality are altered when he dons the cloak of Superman and goes into action. Superman, Batman, and other similar comic book characters have traits linking them to the archetypal hero. The fantasy elements of their abilities can be tracked to ancient myths and folktales. Fairly or unfairly some reviewers have likened Clancy's characters to comic book figures. (According to Clancy's oldest daughter, her father enjoys watching cartoons on television.) Unlike the famed figures of the comics, however, Edwards cannot fly on his own power. Yet his connection to the air force is suggestive, although it is unlikely that this was a conscious choice of the author. Hidden inside Edwards are all the makings of a Superman. Only the right combination of events is needed to bring those superb qualities to the surface.

Without hesitation Edwards takes over, telling the three surviving enlisted men they have a duty to escape and report to friendly forces the results of the Russian attacks on the air base. Revelatory of his innate abilities, he immediately becomes an expert radio operator serving as both eyes and ears to the Allied forces. Because of the intelligence Edwards provides, they are able to track movements of the enemy and send troops to Iceland, as well as to save Edwards and his men.

In a review of *Red Storm Rising*, Robert Lekachman spoke of Clancy's "characterizations" as being "on a Victorian boys' book level" (8). Lekachman doesn't develop the point any further, nor does he identify anyone in particular. However, what he has done, intentionally or not, is to bring to mind features of the early spy stories of the late nineteenth or turn-of-the-century novels. The portrait of Edwards, more than any other man in the book, follows the model of the development of the hero in the adventure/spy fiction of another period in history. Edwards meets one challenge after another with whatever the situation calls for. He shows resolution when he takes charge and sets off into the unknown country with his men. He reveals humor as he puts together his radio for one of his many transmissions: "E. T., phone home" (215). He displays fortitude when faced with little or no food or water, only rain, snow, intense cold. And he is brave beyond the norm.

Edwards rescues a maiden in distress, Vigdis, a young Icelandic woman who is being gang-raped by Soviet soldiers when the Americans come upon her family's farmhouse. With the saving of Vigdis and both the hot and cold vengeance the men take on the enemy Edwards's transformation is complete. The heroic code requires that he kill those men who have violated Vigdis, but not the Russians who were prevented from doing so. Although Edwards sentences all of them to death according to the Uniform Code of Military Justice, it is one of the enlisted men that follows through and does the dirty work. In the convention of the traditional thriller, the hero must perform only noble acts, as Edwards does in revenging the violation of the maiden. For Edwards to perform the action might diminish his heroic stature. His role as leader and commander is also solidified with his men, gaining him their absolute respect through these deeds. He becomes "Skipper" to them at last. At the end of the novel, still true to the formula, Edwards and the maiden fall in love. Comic strip or fairy tale style, a happy future is assured for them in marriage.

Narrative Strategies and the Function of the Hero

Writing about Edwards's role in the novel, Walter Hixson speaks of "the rape and subsequent rescue" of Vigdis as a revival of a "narrative formula." That formula first appeared in "James Fenimore Cooper's Leatherstocking Tales and [was] cemented in American cultural discourse ever since." In a type of mythology similar to Cooper's, Iceland becomes for Edwards a frontier that must be controlled. The frontier myths of Cooper turn on "scenes of captivity, savagery, and violent re-generation through the heroism of the solitary hunter." Hixson believes the passages in *Red Storm Rising* that cover the episodes of rape and its aftermath are part of an underlying American vision of all enemies as bestial adversaries (610).

Where Hixson focuses on Edwards's role in the playing out of cultural myths, Andrew Williams in *T. E. Notes* describes a totally different inspiration for the portrayal of the young meteorologist. Williams believes that Clancy deliberately drew Edwards to resemble the heroic Englishman T. E. Lawrence, familiar to readers and moviegoers as Lawrence of Arabia. Williams finds more than half a dozen traits in common between the two men: names, Thomas Edward Lawrence and Michael D. Edwards; size, small and slight; careers—T. E. also began as a lieutenant; abilities of many kinds, most importantly leadership; training—T. E. at first was a map maker; and the degradation of rape. Whether Williams or Hixson is close to Clancy's intentions in the portrait and development of Edwards, the young lieutenant is the only American in the novel who provides any narrative interest for the reader. The others have too much sameness.

Soviet Characters

A problem of sameness also exists in most of Clancy's Soviet characters. The ordinary soldier is admirable. He does his duty, defends what he believes to be his country's just cause, and fights against all odds. In essence, he is like the American GI. But that is not true of the politicians. Most of them are stick figures, "bad guys" with no redeeming traits. Only a few are more complex. Of these, the Russian general who is most important is Pavel Leonidovich Alexseyev. He is a great tactician who has his first combat experience in the initial breakthrough in the West. With knowledge broadened by combat he fights hard to fulfill his assigned mission, and his role becomes more and more significant to the outcome of the war. Alexseyev is a man who loves his country more than politics. Trained throughout his life to follow orders whether he agrees with them or not, he struggles between loyalty to a cause in which he doesn't believe and the welfare of all the Soviet people. His wisdom far outweighs that of his superiors although for a long time he bows to the system, both military and political. Ultimately, he chooses the "right" path and in so doing salvages what he can.

A curious parallel exists between the development of the young American, Edwards, and the older, established Russian, Alexseyev. Military events shape both their lives, and their choices and actions are vital to the welfare of their country. Their selflessness affects the outcome of the war. Although they never meet and they differ in background, training, lifestyle, and experience, at the core there is a bond, the bond of heroism. In bringing these two men to the forefront of the actions, the writer suggests that good men exist on both sides of the battle line, even if the cause of one is totally without merit.

STYLE

Red Storm Rising resembles Clancy's first-published novel stylistically and philosophically. Both plots depend on technology, but far greater use is made of it in this novel. No machinery used or developed for modern wars nor technological detail is spared. Aficionados enjoy it tremendously, whereas the nonmilitary reader often is overwhelmed by the terminology. Christopher Lehman-Haupt, reviewing the novel, satirizes Clancy's prose: "It isn't Henry V's eloquence at Agincourt that gets the troops to engage. It's messages like this one: 'Z0357Z15June Fr: Saclanto To: All Saclant ships top secret . . . ' " (C21). Dismissively, Lehman-Haupt finds the book more like a videogame than a novel.

Although the majority of reviewers are critical of the prose, many like James Glassman also find "exciting and edifying high-tech tank battles, undersea chases and aerial dogfights" (4D). Nevertheless, Glassman voices a common complaint about a number of Clancy's novels, commenting there is too much of everything, battles, characters, and locations. Other critics fault the overabundance of subplots. Interviewers and callers on television talk shows sometimes ask the same question about the novels reviewers do—why so much? But not everybody deprecates the length and detail. President Ronald Reagan suggested that *Red Storm Rising* be required reading for people in his administration. When Dan Quayle was a member of the Senate, he claimed that *Red Storm Rising* had an important role in preventing an amendment that would have banned antisatellite weapons.

Few people quarrel with the authenticity of *Red Storm Rising;* yet for sound literary reasons most readers and reviewers rate *The Hunt for Red October* more highly. The stress on weaponry rather than people is much greater in *Red Storm Rising* than in the earlier novel, and the people who do appear are somewhat sketchily drawn and less interesting. Walter Isaacson points out that far too frequently, "Humans are obscured by the afterburn of the weapons system" (64). He feels that not enough pages are given over to the parts he finds most readable, the Iceland segments. Although the Icelandic sections are the only parts of the novel which involve some character development and romance, even those are considered unsatisfactory by some readers. Scott Shuger (a critic scornfully dismissed by Clancy) writes that the author is "lousy at writing scenes between a man and a woman. But he's great at writing sex scenes between a man and a weapons system" (10).

Unfortunately, Clancy has lent substance to gibes of that sort through sensual descriptions of weapons and the affectionate feelings toward them of their operators. The prose used for machines often becomes the language of sex. Further, Clancy has a habit of comparing some of his own, though simulated, military experiences to sex. Shuger gives an example: "And what was his comment after the Army staged mock battles for his viewing pleasure? 'It was Disneyland with guns! It was better than sex!' " (10) And there are other instances.

The reader of this novel might fairly decide that Clancy is more comfortable with ships, planes, and guns than with his characters unless they are in the heat of combat. At such times emotions seem genuinely fresh and uncontrived, the author not influenced by various types of readings. However, when he turns to male-female relationships, whether these take place at home or abroad, the writing becomes pedestrian. Although it was necessary to include human emotions to keep the novel from appearing too much like a composite of military events, Clancy does not seem much interested in them. Only in the Iceland locale does he attempt to do more. There the story line shifts from political and military events to a romantic adventure tale. Among the numerous other subplots, the Icelandic actions are different in that they are military only on the surface. Within the framework of the larger action the personal story takes over. A youth's experiences make him not only a man, but a great hero, rescuer and savior. It exemplifies a basic urmyth—original myths from which others grow—in which the chosen figure goes through all the tests required to become somewhat like a Knight of the Round Table or a demigod.

An odd disjunction occurs between the Iceland scenes and the others, almost as if they are separate works. True, the enemy attacks Iceland as part of its overall strategy, but from that point on the Icelandic episodes stand apart from other actions. In contrast to the quick shifts and fast pace of most of the novel, the slow movements of the surviving Americans in Iceland seem out of sync. For example, in one typical military chapter, an air battle is followed by a scene of tank warfare undergoing an airplane attack, followed by a description of activities and anxieties aboard a convoy, followed by a view of a control station tracking information from satellites. But in Iceland, even as the men (later accompanied by Vigdis) make their cautious way on foot across the unaccommodating terrain, there are memorable images about the landscape. Images also make realistic the efforts of the group to survive climate, lack of food, and enemy actions. These details are a reminder of the author's engaging use of imagery in his first novel.

THEMES

Philosophically, *Red Storm Rising* is linked to the earlier work *Red October*. The same manichean attitudes prevail. A country and its people are either good or bad. There are no gray areas. However, there is one change in this book. The "good" people and countries are not only the United States and its citizens but also its Western allies. In spite of the inclusion of a few right-thinking Russian leaders and dutiful Soviet military men, the enemy is shown as devious, lying, and amoral. Most of them have no concern for their own people, but only for themselves, and they exploit everyone to benefit themselves and their plans. In situation after situation the Soviet political and military figures are revealed to be masters of deception. They play upon trust as well as fear to obtain their own ends. They are willing to kill Soviet children, undercut colleagues, and sacrifice their own men. These things can happen because they are not like Americans, whom they dupe, because Americans are naive. At first the Soviets are successful in their underhanded behavior, but eventually all those acts are revealed and reversed, because Americans, unlike the Soviets, pull together for the benefit of all. Good overcomes evil, and order is restored, if only temporarily. The Soviet Union can never be trusted, as Clancy continues to show in his next novels.

Nowhere is there any consideration or prediction of the fall of communism or the disintegration of the Soviet Union because of economic or political failure. Everything hinges on military strengths or weaknesses. *Red Storm Rising* implies the infallibility of U.S. intelligence services. Given that the dissolution of the Soviet Union was only a few years away from the publication of this novel, one might expect to see some hint of the failure of U.S. intelligence, but there is none.

ALTERNATE READING: PSYCHOANALYTIC CRITICISM

In addition to a close textual analysis, other critical approaches may be taken. Various ways exist to look at the human situation. One popular method is through psychoanalytic reading, based on the work of Sigmund Freud. If we consider some modern versions of Freudian criticism, we find that *Red Storm Rising* and other Clancy novels may be examined in this way.

Anxiety, multiple fears, and an individual's sense of fragmentation are part of the human experience. Naturally, people prefer to ignore fear and seek instead pleasure and gratification. However, we learn from infancy on that pleasure and gratification are limited, perhaps not even allowed in various circumstances. Because some pleasures are taboo or dangerous, the practice of those must be repressed for the good of the individual and society. For any society to function, certain rules of behavior must exist, including repression of actions deemed unhealthy or undesirable. Through the social process children are taught to repress some elements of their nature. That type of repression is learned and a conscious act.

But repression also has another aspect, referred to as unconscious repression. Desires that are unattainable, forbidden, taboo are buried at so deep a level that the individual is unaware of them or unable to bring them to consciousness in any comprehensible way. Freudian analysts refer most frequently to Oedipal, incestuous longings of childhood, but there are other desires as well. In time, children move beyond the Oedipal and successive stages into an acceptance of authority. They develop awareness and acceptance of boundaries, controls, and limits that are considered conscience (what Freud calls the superego). However, guilty longings always exist at the deep unconscious level. The unconscious "is a place and a non-place, which is completely indifferent to reality, which knows no logic or negation or causality or contradiction" (Eagleton 157).

One glimpse of the unconscious comes through dreams, which, according to Freud, provide a form of wish fulfillment. They serve as substitutes for actions. We cannot always understand dreams, because their symbolic images frequently defy interpretation. However, other clues to unconscious desires and feelings come through language, through slips of the tongue, through jokes. Problems faced by an analysand, that is, a patient, sometimes are seen in treatment as transference. Patients may transfer to the analyst the conflicts which have brought them into treatment, problems with parents, spouses, employers, others. At that point the analyst "becomes" the source of the problems, which then may be brought into the open where they can be dealt with. Additionally, psychoanalysis takes into account projection, beliefs that others think, feel, and want what we do.

Freud has stated that the value of psychoanalysis is the replacement of fear with reason and control. Yet, none of this is ever complete. There is always a "split" of some kind between what is conscious and what is repressed. But not only does analysis help with both the release and control of feelings. Art and other forms of culture do that. Not everyone wants, needs, or seeks analytic help. Literature and art may fulfil individual requirements.

Another aspect of psychoanalysis to consider when examining the role literature may play is the Lacanian view of human personality. The psychoanalyst Jacques Lacan—said to rewrite, or reinterpret, Freud—describes what he calls the mirror stage of development. Simply stated, it is the process the child follows in constructing the self by reflecting objects and other persons and identifying with those. Through images, children build an imagined unified self, an image that provides meaning for self. But it is never ending and therefore ever changing as the individual (originally the child, but later the adult) moves from one object or figure to another. There is always "lack" which it is necessary to fill.

Although throughout life most of us find some unity or coherence to ourselves, both Freud and Lacan suggest we are always attempting to unify the split, to construct the unified coherent self. By identifying with certain objects we gain a feeling of satisfaction, of unity that is like a complete circle. Literature, in addition to its other functions, also serves as the object which helps provide the sense of completion, which fills in the "lack," the spaces in the personality.

All literature sets into play our unconscious fantasies, our fears, and desires. Often, it has been argued by critics, suspense/thriller stories, more than any other form of writing arouse these feelings. It is in the nature of the genre to stimulate hidden worries as well as longings. However, this type of fiction also assuages such buried emotions, emotions that are often disguised in dreams or nightmares. Characters, landscapes, buildings appear in forms that represent yet hide those materials one fears to confront. Thriller fiction permits them to surface in an acceptable form, providing satisfaction unlike the results from other forms of fiction. Thrillers have their own different motivation, frequently different audiences, and usually different results.

Perhaps the popularity of thriller literature results from its service to psychological needs. There is variance in these needs, but what all readers want is a combination of "safe" involvement in danger and reassurance as the end result. *Red Storm Rising* does that, in bringing to the surface fears Americans hold as individuals as well as those of an entire nation. Clancy's novel also provides ways of transforming anxieties into acceptable and even positive feelings. The most obvious concern he deals with is worry about a future war, all kinds of warfare, weapons, not the least of which are nuclear or chemical, and defeat, obliteration, death. He names the enemy of the day, in this and several other books, the Soviets. He touches on all that the reader believes rightly or wrongly about the Russian character and creates the most fearsome situations that such an enemy will engage in from the impersonal to the personal. The novel tells us our suspicions are justified, with the result that the United States enters an all-out war. Our military forces constantly prepare for such an event. Their readiness is demonstrated. The United States is powerful everywhere in the world, as demonstrated by Desert Storm, the Persian Gulf War in the early 1990s.

Although at times it seems that the forces of darkness, the enemy, will win, the "good guys" in Clancy invariably overcome them. The situation is idealized in that it is not fact but a construct. As readers we participate in the actions, the danger, the fear of disfigurement, of death. Even as our heart and blood race, we enjoy our situation, reassured by the text that we are an invincible people. That is part of the contract we have with entertainment thrillers, and with this novel. They provide us heroic actions as we become the heroes who man planes, lead convoys, destroy subs and satellites. In the novel, unlike in fearful dream or perhaps actual situations, we are powerful, with the feeling that the world is centered on us. When tested, we overcome all odds. We are never cowards. Even if we lose one action, we return to the fray. Others may die. We will not, because the tacit contract guarantees personal invulnerability. *Red Storm Rising* promises and delivers victory.

The novel similarly unveils other secret fears, and desires are treated in a similar manner. Although worry about rape is primarily female fear of violation, masculine anxiety has to do with protection of one's women. Is it possible to keep them from harm? Edwards, our surrogate in the novel, was once unable to save the woman he loved, but the score is evened out later in a replication of the earlier events. It is almost like a dream in its transformational power.

Can we avenge violent acts with our own code of justice? *Red Storm Rising* answers in the affirmative. Is it possible to restore harmony? Here too we are comforted. Readers know we must lose something. In the novel, not only are lives lost (other people's), but also lost is a form of innocence, a reminder that something must be sacrificed for a better life to be found. We are purged in this type of fiction when recovery takes place and we return, in a sense, to a safe haven. That is what we knew would happen.

5

Patriot Games
(1987)

There is often a difficult child who gets the most attention in a family. Among Clancy's novels *Patriot Games* fills that role. He told interviewer Jean Ross: "It was the hardest one to write" (111). Perhaps it was most difficult because, although it was the third one published, it was the first novel Clancy wrote. With his introduction here to the Jack Ryan stories he began to develop the hero "whose character was really formed in the first chapter" of the book "which was written in 1978 or so" (111). Surprisingly, Clancy informed Ross he spent three weeks on research for the novel, more time on research than on any of his other fiction (up to 1989). Most readers would automatically assume his more technical novels would have required greater preparation, but apparently not.

Although Clancy as recently as 1992 proclaimed *Patriot Games* his favorite work, the public has not taken to it as well as his other novels. Sales figures, reputedly in the neighborhood of 800,000 for the hardcover edition, would have been considered excellent for almost any other publication. Still, those numbers do not match the millions for Clancy's earlier or later books. How can we account for the disparities in the response of the public? Reviews for all his work have been similar in both their praise and criticism. The kudos—exciting though unlikely plot, shared human emotions. The negatives—simplistic morality, dull characters. As seems the case for everything Clancy has written, opinion remains divided about reasons for readership appeal. Ross Thomas, book critic for the *New York Times,* suggests there are circumscribed types of audiences for the author's fiction. *Patriot Games,* he states, "should quite please those who, given the choice, will pick steadfast black and white over doubtful gray every time" (11). What he doesn't say is that group consists of the largest number of readers in the world. Furthermore, with the publication of this third novel, Clancy reached the name recognition of longtime famous thriller writers. John McCarthy, in the *National Review,* compares *Patriot Games* favorably to novels by the writer Clancy most admires, Frederick Forsythe, "in its lively description of highly technical activity such as implanting explosives or viewing reconnaissance-satellite photography" (53).

PLOT DEVELOPMENT

Clancy thinks this novel very much a love story, but it is unlikely that most readers would characterize it that way. Yet, neither can the label "technothriller" be applied, for unlike any other Clancy novel this one has little of a technological nature. In most ways the generic pattern is that of spy/espionage thriller. The plot focuses on terrorism, a familiarly appalling activity in the British Isles. For the first time in history, though, those operations are transported to the United States.[1] While Americans might expect the terrorists to be members of the Irish Republican Army (IRA), they are not. Rather, this is a fictional group the author names the ULA, acronym for the Ulster Liberation Army. The imaginary ULA is described as a branch of the actual Provisional Irish Republican Army, whose acronym is PIRA and which is also called Provos for short. Provos, the Marxist segment of the IRA, separated from the parent body in the 1970s. It is the Provos who have committed acts of terrorism in Northern Ireland and England, anti-British and anti-Protestant activities. The hostilities between various Catholic and Protestant groups have been called "the troubles." Historically, part of the Irish-American community has given financial support to the IRA, a point made in the novel, in which an Irish-American tavern carries the name of Patriots Club, not because of its affection for America but for Ireland.

Clancy's fictional group of terrorists is a small but fanatic Maoist offshoot of the Provos, their bitter enemy. Both groups are violent, the real and the imaginary one, but in the novel the Ulster Liberation Army is singled out by a British intelligence officer when he contemptuously labels them "nasty buggers" (30). Each terrorist organization spies on the other, hoping to see it eliminated.

When the story opens, in London, members of ULA have killed a chauffeur driving the automobile of the prince and princess of Wales and their infant son. Their kidnapping plan is foiled by the fortuitous intervention of Jack Ryan, who becomes involved in a shootout with the terrorists. Although at the moment of the attack Ryan has no knowledge of the royal occupants of the vehicle, he responds as a marine-trained officer to what is clearly a terrorist act. The royals are frightened but uninjured, unlike Ryan, who is severely wounded in the episode. An important ULA assassin, Sean Miller, survives but is captured by the police. He goes to prison whereas Ryan is transported to the hospital.

For his actions, various members of the royal family show their gratitude to Ryan. The queen and the duke of Edinburgh as well as their son, the prince of Wales, visit him in the hospital and see to it that the rescuing hero receives VIP treatment. Ryan's wife and child are recipients of British hospitality at Buckingham Palace, and Ryan is made a knight of the Royal Victorian Order. From that point on, the British refer to him as Sir John. After his recovery, Ryan, his now newly pregnant wife, and their young daughter, Sally, return to the United States, where Jack again takes up his job teaching at the U.S. Naval Academy in Annapolis and Cathy her work as an ophthalmic surgeon.

They believe that their life will resume its former peaceful existence. Predictably, they are wrong. The terrorists want vengeance, as well as another chance to kidnap the prince and princess when they make an expected visit to the United States. Ryan also is a major target, second only to the Waleses. Unbeknownst to anyone for some period of time after the cleverly arranged and brutal escape of Sean Miller from custody, the ULA makes its plans for action abroad. Miller and his cohorts train in the country of Chad for the coming attack in America, while Ryan and his family remain unaware of the threat. Kevin O'Donnell, the Irish head of the ULA organization, joins Miller and his group, along with greedy, anarchistic American thugs in an attempt to carry out their violent plans.

After British and American operatives alert Ryan to the possibility of ULA attacks on him, he takes several defensive steps. This includes weapons training at the Academy and greater involvement at the CIA, where he is able to learn more about the terrorists. But the enemy group has planned well and carefully, so that for a time it seems they will succeed in their mission. Everything falls into place for them in their initial attempts on the lives of Cathy and Sally Ryan, as well as later in their attack on the Ryan home during the royal visit. But again Ryan saves the day—and the lives of his family and guests. In an action-packed trip on the Chesapeake Bay he, with a little help from his friends, one of whom is the prince of Wales, overtakes and captures the two leading terrorists (whose fate will be settled in a future book). Ryan's reward in the tense conclusion is the birth of a son, Jack, Jr.

CHARACTERS

Terrorists

In his portrayal of the Irish terrorists, Clancy is far less rigid than he has been until now with Russian enemies. Where his Russian characters, with some notable exceptions, are stereotypically evil men, the ULA members have greater depth. As a result of the writer's creative efforts at individualization, they are people more easily remembered. Of course it helps that there are fewer of them than in Clancy's normally large cast. He doesn't expend time on lesser ULA figures. It is sufficient to let the reader know they exist and then focus on the significant players. The Irish anarchists are even more vicious than the worst Russians Clancy has depicted, though equally indifferent to human lives, even among the Irish. The terrorists' hatred runs more deeply. Theirs is more personal, fiercer, and less calculated than the Russians'. Perhaps that is why they are more realistic and therefore more believable than the large number of flat, evil Russians of the first two novels.

Is it that Clancy, an Irish-American Catholic has genuine sympathy for the situation of Irish Catholics, in spite of his affection and admiration for the British? Or, is it as one critic has remarked, that the Irish terrorist, the single-minded, cold Sean Miller is another kind of "Clancy ideal," his "dark familiar, his *Doppelganger*, the armed and dangerous one . . . all that Clancy is not. Disorderly, unmilitary, reckless, anarchic" (Ryan 37–38). This statement suggests that Miller represents the ominous and secret "other" for Clancy, a buried self that analysts tell us exists for all of us, our hidden heart of darkness.

Miller, surely the complete opposite of the knowable Clancy, also stands at the far end of the spectrum from Ryan, the hero in whom the author admittedly sees himself. (Although the author has pointed to his deliberate doubling with Ryan, undoubtedly he would deny the doubling with the assassin Miller. Not only does he object to most literary analysis but also to psychologizing.) Through Jack Ryan's musings, Clancy makes the point that terrorists can't be identified among other average citizens. In appearance Miller is nondescript, no different, Ryan thinks, than an executive in training for an investment firm. If we were searching for a villain or a hero, we would be more inclined to notice Ryan than the younger, shorter, thinner Miller. But Miller has one very memorable feature: his eyes.

The pale gray eyes become the focus of the description. If eyes are the window of the soul, as Ralph Waldo Emerson thought, Miller's soul is an empty shell. The eyes hold nothing. No human spark comes from those eyes. Ryan and all the British who have dealt with Miller regard him as an animal. On trial for murder he resembles a caged wolf, a predator with no human qualities. He spares nobody whom he regards as an enemy or who interferes with his plans, even if they have been decent to him. When a police officer, who had rescued him after he'd been sodomized in prison, reminds him of the act as Miller coldly shoots him, Miller responds with a quote from Joseph Stalin: "Gratitude . . . is a disease of dogs" (189).

The frightening single-mindedness of Miller is disquieting for the reader, fitting all we have read and heard of terrorists. He is what we fear in the dark of night, the amoral hunter, bomber, the killer without a conscience. To reach his goal, he will not hesitate to destroy anyone, including little children. Miller is henchman to the equally fanatic, but better educated and more controlled ULA leader, Kevin O'Donnell. Once a member of the Provos, O'Donnell coldly eliminated a large number of his cohorts because he disagreed with their political views. He is a man who, like many actual spies, has a legitimate daily cover for his terrorist operations. His organization has functioned well because O'Donnell has been able to recruit two types of anarchists, those people who commit violent acts and those who provide information that fuels those acts. His espionage ring has even penetrated the palace, where an aide to the queen is a secret member of ULA. These characters stir post–World War II memories of history for us, when men close to the British throne were revealed to be agents for the USSR.

One of the ULA spies, Dennis Cooley, the Irish owner of a London bookstore, is a clone of a Graham Greene figure in *The Human Factor*. (This may well be an unconscious imitation on Clancy's part, a reminder of critic Harold Bloom's theory about anxiety and influence, but nevertheless there. Bloom theorizes that literature is always a reworking of

some earlier literature.) The two bookstore owners have similar functions, engage in many of the same actions, and up to a point appear
interchangeable. Not only is neither suspected of spying, but both thor-
oughly innocuous men are antithetical to any stereotypical conception of
leftist agents. They are quiet, with extremely reserved demeanor,
thoughtful, cautious, knowledgeable dealers in antique books. When the
time requires them to take action, each does so. At that point, however,
Clancy's spy, Cooley, becomes a totally different person, with no resemblance to Greene's.

Thought of as "a bloody cipher, a zero" and "a nerd" (363) by British
intelligence agents before they learn the truth about his activities, Cooley
turns into a vengeful and violent man once his cover is blown and his
old, secret but pleasurable life comes to an end. He insists on becoming
part of the group of ULA assassins training in Chad for the attack in
America. If ever a man, actual or fictional, had a Hydean personality,
Cooley is that person. His hatred, says the omniscient author, is like acid
eating at him. The reader accepts and understands that, but there is a
problem with the personality changes that take place so abruptly. Although all the terrorists are cruel fanatics, the heretofore controlled Cooley (one should note the irony of the name) becomes the most
emotionally involved, even more than Miller in his fury. Gone is the
bland, cautious, quiet-speaking bookseller. In his place appears a foul-
mouthed, racist brute. Such abrupt alterations belong to the genre of
horror stories or films, not espionage novels. The portrait of Cooley
would have been far better had it remained close to that of Greene's
man.

The American Hero

If Sean Miller personifies the role of the dark "other," Ryan represents
the ideal, the fantasized heroic self, not only for the author but also for
Clancy's ideal reader. In *Patriot Games* Ryan's life lines are established.
A general biography provides structure for future events, which are seen
in the first published novel, *Hunt for Red October*. In the pattern of an
archetypal hero (first model from which later heroes stem), Ryan quickly
displays his strengths and virtues, beginning the long sequence of exploits that test his mettle.

The audience that wants details about Ryan should read *Patriot Games*
first. Although it isn't necessary to have more information to understand

the story line of *Red October* (as noted in chapter 4, Ryan does not appear in *Red Storm Rising*), it would probably add interest to the reading. Whether the author intended it or not when he first began to write, Ryan became a series hero following the success of the first book. Each experience is a building block for later novels that include Ryan and have references along the way to other adventures. Through the use of multiple conversations in *Patriot Games* the writer provides the reader with Ryan's biography, his family background, schooling, and military experience. Clancy as all-knowing author also provides entrée into the character's thoughts. In the first few pages of the book we learn more about Ryan than in all of *Red October*. He drives a five-year-old Volkswagen Rabbit, a point Clancy apparently considers an important reflection of Ryan's taste, since he mentions it twice (13, 172). Ryan has a photographic memory (like the author). And he doesn't like crowds. Wherever possible, Clancy seizes opportunities to build Ryan's strong image and contrasting modesty: "The Marines taught you to shoot very well indeed," a British detective observes. Ryan, however, credits his late father for that, and in passing makes himself seem like just any average person holding a gun: "Anyway, the guy (an assassin) was only fifteen feet away" (44).

If Ryan is reticent about his achievements, his creator is not. Clancy doesn't skimp on praise for his model character. Everyone who works with Ryan learns to value him beyond measure. A highly placed member of the CIA wants Ryan to work for the Agency, telling him: "The Agency needs people like you, Jack. You've got a feel for things. You don't think and act like a bureaucrat. You say what you think. Not everyone in this building does that" (445). Given what the public learned of CIA failings in 1994, Clancy again seems prescient, although the CIA is rarely a target for his attacks. Ryan represents the type of man the author would like to serve in all government positions.

But seeing more of Ryan, as we do in this novel, does not necessarily improve the image the author intends. Greater visibility fails to make Ryan as appealing as the writer suggests, at least until we are well into the book. In the first segment of the work Ryan has a clumsy, untutored aspect that grates. Though said to be a wonder boy, nothing about him, except his being quick on the draw in the early part of the novel, reinforces the idea. All kinds of terms come to mind in attempting to describe the impression he makes on the reader: country bumpkin, bull in a china shop, cowboy *and* Indian, Mr. Smith goes to London.

Ryan has a gee-whiz quality about him all the time he is in Britain, and whenever we see him there, he has the demeanor of a gaping, rubber-necking tourist. After all, his wife has been to Britain a number of times and must have talked of it. He is working and vacationing in that country and ought not to be astonished by what he sees, the driving practices, the elegant cars, the weather, or the living style and customs of royalty. In *Patriot Games* the clothes he wears easily identify him as an American. When seen at a later date in *The Hunt for Red October* his suits say Savile Row, so that at least outwardly he changes with time. Ryan is starstruck, but not tongue-tied, and his sense of awe about being with the aristocracy never keeps him from dispensing advice freely to members of the royal family. As a result, his speech patterns are a strange mixture of deference and familiarity in relationship to the Windsors and the Waleses.

Once he returns home, however, his behavior alters significantly, and for the better. He becomes more surefooted in all ways, and even some of the dialogue improves, no doubt because he and Clancy are on familiar ground at the Naval Academy, the CIA, with friends much like themselves. His marine training becomes even more important in the United States than in England. Thus, when he must once again protect the prince and princess as well as his own family, he becomes a cold, calculating killer enraged by the attacks on those he loves. And although he proves himself a man of strength and action whenever and wherever necessary, he seems more of a hero in the United States.

The Hero's Wife

Unlike her role in *Red Storm Rising*, here Cathy Ryan has an important part in the plot line. When the ULA assassins come to America, they attempt to kill her and her daughter to revenge themselves on Ryan. The plan backfires, and worse than that, makes Ryan himself a different man from the one he was before. Though Cathy cannot abide violence, she understands why Jack must become a killer. He is man; she is woman. Once again revealing his limitations in depicting female characters, Clancy puts Cathy's thoughts into the most banal language. About pregnancy: "She knew she was a woman, doing something Jack could neither duplicate nor fully comprehend" (425). Hardly the level of thought a reader might expect from a trained surgeon. At times, thinking about Jack, she refers to him as "my man," words that have more the flavor of a blues ballad than the thoughts of the independent, take-charge woman of the London segments of the novel. Where the depiction of Jack improves on home territory, that is not true of Cathy. Neither the dialogue nor inner thoughts nor comments about her work change her from the stock, uninteresting characterization. Making her a surgeon does not alter the impression.

Cathy Ryan's youth was a much more privileged one than her husband's. She always drove a Porsche as a girl and continues to do so after marriage, although the Ryans also own a station wagon for convenience. When Ryan wonders why two adults need three cars, she finds amusement in what she sees as Jack's "working-class" attitudes. It entertains her that he worries about what their maid will think if he doesn't tidy up nights before she is to come to work. The reader gets the impression Ryan has married above his station. If not, then why the frequent references to his father-in-law's criticism of him? The two men dislike each other intensely, and Ryan appears to have a need to prove himself constantly to Cathy's father. In several passages of interior monologue, Ryan defends himself angrily, insisting on his ability to take care of Cathy and of measuring up to social and financial standards her father expects. If, as we have been led to believe through interviews with the author, Ryan is his alter-ego, are we being given some biographical insight about Clancy's own relationships? Clancy did work in his in-laws' business before he became a published author, earning large sums of money just as Jack Ryan does.

Minor Characters

There are other characters in the book, mostly male, who play a role in Ryan's growing ability to defeat the Irish assassins. Quite deliberately, Clancy draws two totally opposite African-American men. One is navy pilot Robby Jackson, a superhero and patriot, a devoted friend to Ryan, willing to risk his life for him. (Jackson has a role in several Clancy novels.) The other man is Alex Dobbens, an electrical engineer who seems to have no real reason to betray his country, other than the satisfaction of being a terrorist. Dobbens is a malcontent, an anarchist, clever, skillful, and completely without moral fiber. Because Clancy chose to depict the two men as black, the obvious contrast in personalities leads the reader to speculate about his reasons. The Irish assassins show only contempt for blacks, even their own hireling, who has been paid to help in planning and organizing a large part of the action against

the Ryans and the royals. Through episodes of violent actions and vi-
tuperative language, the author implies that the prejudice of foreigners
far outweighs that of Americans. The ULA members, who are fanatic
followers of communist doctrine, see no contradiction between their political beliefs and their dislike for black people. No attempt is made to
disguise their racism. Sean Miller despises and resents Dobbens. It is he
who kills him.

STYLE: RYAN AS CLANCY'S SPOKESMAN

Patriot Games contains much less technology than the first two published books. What there is sometimes appears in bits and pieces. However, some technological material builds suspense and helps advance the
plot, particularly the parts providing details about reconnaissance satellites. To fill out the pages of the novel the author adds many homely
touches, some of little or no interest because of their ordinariness and
banality. Often they work against the element of suspense by deflecting
attention from the action. Included are passages that add to our knowledge of both author and major character but have no other real function.
Ryan, we learn, has had a superior education, a Jesuit education like
Clancy's—Clancy at Loyola, Ryan at Georgetown. Because of that, a Jesuit priest is brought into the story to provide an opportunity for a short
lecture on the importance and influence of the Jesuits. "No one was
better qualified for this [advice giving] than a Jesuit, meticulously educated, well versed in the ways of the world, but not spoiled by it—most
of the time" (378). Jesuit education builds men "for others," and Ryan
is manifestly one of those men. Nevertheless, Ryan, again like Clancy, is
exceedingly prickly about real or implied criticism. An unspoken response of Ryan's to a conversation: "Happy with what he was, and [he]
didn't need a bunch of amateur pshrinks [sic] . . . to define his personality for him" (105). Because similar statements appear in other Clancy
writings and interviews, they should be read as reflections of the author's
personal feelings.

Typically, Clancy introduces the Jesuit priest for a short description
and discussion, but then drops him from any further consideration, as
he does many characters. Often these minor appearances seem to exist
only for the author to display his learning or to provide a teaching experience of some sort. One example is the surgeon who saves the lives
of Cathy and Sally Ryan and knows about and loathes the work of Edgar

Allan Poe. He calls the poet "a scribbler of death and perversity," a "son of a bitch," whose home in Baltimore is "a demi-shrine for the local literati" (314). One can almost see Clancy's lip curl over the word "literati." However, what is unclear is the reason for this detailed description of a character, the surgeon, who has no further role in the story.

Didactic statements and short lectures also slow the movement of the plot. At times, the author slips into a dictionary mode: "A horsehair wig, called a 'peruke' " (114); "A police officer—they call them constables over here" (12). Although the effect of the technique is like that of a lesson taught by a teacher to an elementary school student, it is moderated by the addition of words such as "he reminded himself" or "he had been told." Still, they give the effect of talking down to the reader. However, when the author eliminates the earnest preachiness of some material, much of the writing becomes enjoyable thriller reading. Much of it is "filler" material.

Because thriller novels have a limited number and a basic sameness of plots, the appeal must come from other sources, from filler. Scholars note that filler material is central to attracting and holding the audience. Sometimes the filler attraction is a look at a glittering world outside ordinary possibilities of experience. Sometimes it is a pleasurable reminder of places we've been to, of events we can recapture through the printed page. Although most of the attention given to Clancy's work comes from his use of technology, much of the appeal of his writing is in his skillful use of filler when he doesn't burden it with personal commentary. As always, he pulls the reader into the novel with a strong opening and a trained eye for imagery. He notes details of architecture, furniture, clothing, landscape. He brings us into a British courtroom, the Tower of London, Heathrow Airport, takes us boating on the Chesapeake in a storm and through buildings new and old of Georgetown University.

THEMES

That the author has strong beliefs may be seen in the themes of all his novels. One does not have to search for themes. They are readily available. Clancy's views about American terrorists, rebels, revolutionaries, or rioters are reflected by the musings of an FBI agent: "America was a hard place to see the benefits of Marxism or Nazism. When even welfare families had color televisions, how much attraction could there be to collectivism? When the country lacked a system of class distinctions, what group could one hate with conviction?" (358). Sociologists, economists, and historians might find much to quarrel with so reductive an analysis of American life. Clancy's own Horatio Alger type of success may have put a mote in his eye, although he did write this novel before he left the world of the insurance business for the more exciting one of fame, fortune, and adulation. Nevertheless, the philosophy behind all his books remains the same. Work and you will succeed. Even if you don't become a millionaire, you are better off than people anywhere else in the world.

Clancy has drawn the policeman's son, Jack Ryan, to exemplify the achievement of the American Dream. All things are possible, he tells us. In what seems almost an unconscious parody of Lewis Carroll's line from *Alice in Wonderland,* "a cat may look at a king," he draws a Camelot in Britain, to which the Ryan family gains entrance. Into the glittering, elegant, luxurious life of no less than the queen and her consort the Ryans are taken as caring friends. No need for the royals to sing "What Do the Simple Folk Do?"—for they are shown as the simplest of simple folk. They may live in total luxury, have affairs of state to concern them and courtiers to help in every aspect of their lives, but at heart and in speech they are just as humble and ordinary as the rest of us. Beneath the skin, according to one of Clancy's themes, good people are the same.

Ryan seems committed to treating the royals as next-door neighbors. Planning a regular folks' meal of steak, potatoes, and salad to serve the prince and princess when they visit the Ryan home, Jack informs his wife: "Everywhere they go over here, people will be hitting them with that fancy French crap. Somebody ought to give them a decent American meal" (450). American food, like all things American, is superior. On the arrival of the royals at Peregrine Cliff, the Ryan house, "As usually happened, the people immediately split into male and female groups" (481). In gender grouping, Clancy-style, the royals are no different from down-to-earth Americans. The dinner party, before the terrorist action interrupts it, is as casual as Cathy and Sally's stay at Buckingham Palace, where the queen behaves much like a fond, middle-class nanny.

ALTERNATE READING: THE NOVEL AS A FAIRY TALE

Patriot Games differs from the earlier Clancy novels not only in the limited amount of technology but also in the inclusion of a number of intimate scenes and conversations between the Ryans. The author's reference to the novel as a love story opens the way to multiple types of reading, as do the romantic and sexual episodes. One theoretical reading is to look at the novel as a modern fairy tale. Many novelistic patterns, including those of thrillers, go back not only to the fairy tale but even to the earlier folktale. Components of both of these were incorporated into certain types of adventure stories and later into spy/suspense/thriller stories. These ingredients include danger to country and individuals, love, battle, rescue, and reward. Although spy/espionage novels appear very realistic because they have a number of familiar elements from life, and sometimes actual events, there is a considerable amount of fantasy in them.

English and American adventure, thriller, and spy novels novels are the forerunners of *Patriot Games* in multiple ways, not the least of which is in their simplification of the complexities of the world. Problems are shrunk and reduced to confrontation between the right side and the wrong side. No hidden layers beneath the surface nor shadowy areas disturb the distinct differences. This simplicity, which comes from the fairy tale, can be seen in nineteenth-and early twentieth-century writers such as Sapper (pseudonym for H. C. McNeile), James Fenimore Cooper, John Buchan, and Ian Fleming. Such simplicity remains a part of some thriller/espionage fiction today. Although the complexities of the technology in Clancy's fiction might lead the reader to think of the work as complex, many other aspects are as basic as the fairy tale.

When boundaries between good and evil are clear, choices may be made easily. What was a somewhat vague land in the fairy tale becomes our side, our country in the thriller. Clancy's division between "us," or our country, and "them," or their country, may be seen as a development from the fairy tale. Invasions by hostile men in early tales becomes the force of Irish terrorism, the ULA in *Patriot Games*. Fairy tales are generally set within monarchical kingdoms, which naturally reject any other type of rule. In the modern world there have been different "isms," among them fascism and communism. What was the "bad" character or group in the fairy tale becomes in Clancy and many modern thrillers the evil communist group seeking to destroy capitalism.

Patriot Games focuses initially on the British monarchy and its struggle against the hostile, destructive force, the terrorists, that would bring it down. Later, in a fairy-tale pattern, the struggle becomes a fight (much like a duel) to the death between the hero and the dark force. Issues of duty, sacrifice, loyalty, and disloyalty important in the fairy tale are equally important in modern thrillers, not only for the political agenda but also for the portrait of the modern hero. The contemporary hero beneath his facade is not much different from the rescuing knight of early tales.

One road sign to our reading of the novel as a fairy tale has to do with the regal cast of queen, consort, prince, princess, and infant heir. Harmony and love are part of the mythical kingdom and of Britain (another unfortunate anachronism in Clancy's fiction, given recent revelations about the marriage of the gallant prince and beautiful princess of Wales). Evil men abound, in the mythical past and present, seeking to take over the kingdom, to decimate the happy land and replace it with their own dark rule. Although in *Patriot Games* violence occurs outside the palace, a villain works within it to destroy the monarchy. The villain may appear in one guise as a loyal follower of the monarchs. Yet, secretly he is like the worm within that comes in the night to destroy the monarchy. Because stability depends on heirs, the plot here is based largely on the danger to the young royals and their baby son and later on the danger to still another family, the Ryans.

Like a fairy tale, on the surface all is pomp and circumstance, elegance and luxury, but danger lurks everywhere. When a formidable hero is needed to save the succession, Jack Ryan appears. First, however, the hero must be tested, as Ryan is, becoming instantly recognizable as superior when he puts himself in mortal danger by saving the royals. That is only the beginning of a series of testing situations, characteristic of a fairy tale. The enemy lives on. Thus, in accordance with mythical legends, Ryan must prove himself again with the same opponent. Recognizable as a modern-day St. George, he succeeds in slaying the dragons who would destroy everything he values. Guards of the fairy-tale kingdom give way to soldiers and policemen in the modern thriller, and dungeons become prisons. Swords are replaced with guns, and horses with boats, but the results are the same, victory.

In traditional fairy tales the hero is rewarded by marrying the princess he has rescued. No bedroom scenes take the reader beyond the marriage ceremony. In modern thrillers, however, the hero is rewarded with sex. So too is Jack Ryan. Although it is a more sedate version of sex (marital, in Clancy novels, though not in most other thrillers), nonetheless, the motif is the same. Released from the English hospital, cast on his arm, he is escorted by the duke of Edinburgh to a party in his honor at Buckingham Palace. There he and his wife spend the night, and Ryan behaves like the invincible hero he is. He and his wife make love. As with that fantasy hero, James Bond, Ryan's nearly fatal injuries never interfere with the sexual reward.

NOTE

1. Since the publication of the novel, terrorism has become a reality also in the United States.

The Cardinal of the Kremlin
(1988)

With the publication of Clancy's fourth novel, reviewers began to speak of his books less as the fare of presidents than as the vacationer's escapist reading. The novels are "something of a summer ritual, each hitting the bookstores just in time to be snatched up and tossed in the beach bag along with the huarache sandals and the aloe vera." The new book is "a perfect accompaniment to the music of sand and surf," writes Andrew Ferguson (101). In *Time* John Skow describes the novel as airplane fare which will "blot(s) out the realities of baggage deprivation and child-size seats." Is *The Cardinal of the Kremlin* a significant and influential political thriller? Skow suggests not, only that it is superior to *Patriot Games*, which he says was "a frippery . . . even sillier than real life." The latest Clancy work "is precisely as silly as real life." The reader shouldn't consider the book substantive, he indicates, but it serves a purpose for those of us who (presumably like Skow and Clancy) have a fear of flying: "For the duration of the flight," anyhow, it "is less strenuous and far more reassuring" than white-knuckle flying (EB3).

Do these rather breezy reviews suggest the book is a lightweight undertaking? The evaluation seems to depend in large measure on the reader's and writer's belief in or rejection of the Strategic Defense Initiative, (SDI), flippantly named Star Wars by critics. The SDI was a proposal to develop an antiballistic missile defense system. That program, which is the impetus for the book, in reality was never built. *The Cardinal of the*

Kremlin was published at the end of Ronald Reagan's term, by which time interest in SDI was considerably diminished. No hint of that exists in the book. Nevertheless, with the presidential changing of the guard, readership for Clancy's fiction still included two aficionados in the highest offices of the land. One was President George Bush, who said that Clancy's contribution was a "marvelous" one "to our literary world and, I also would like to think, to the national security interests of the United States." And the other was Vice President Dan Quayle, who found Clancy's work to be more influential than other novels. "They're read as the real thing," he asserted (Shuger 11).

By 1988–89 critics often disagreed with that assessment, a few even to the point of questioning the author's use of "high-tech jargon." Clancy may "delve(s) into Star Wars weaponry, but murkily" (Novak 37). Reviews by then were very much in accord with the judgments of Ferguson and Skow. In paging through various types of writings about Clancy and his work from the late eighties onward, the reader begins to sense that Clancy's novels are assuming their rightful place as thrillers and spy novels rather than political punditry. Whereas reviewers intuit the shift without analyzing the reasons behind changes of attitudes, longer and more scholarly articles evaluate both the author and his material much more critically. Nevertheless, the concensus among book reviewers is that the new work, *The Cardinal of the Kremlin*, variously labeled a "megatech spy thriller," a "technothriller," or just plain "thriller," is a page turner. Some have called it Clancy's best novel. And, as James Graves observes in the *Conservative Digest*, "Here's excitement" (65).

PLOT DEVELOPMENT

Typical of all his novels, Clancy has a number of plots and subplots advancing simultaneously. For a time each seems to be spinning in its own orbit. But, as always, the author eventually makes clear the interrelationships of the parts, pulling them together for an exhilarating, satisfying, and surprisingly moving ending.

The first plot is introduced as the book opens with scenes from Afghanistan, during the Afghan/Russian war of 1978–88. In that area of central Asia, bands of determined but poorly equipped Afghan guerrillas are attempting to drive the Russians out of their country, killing them wherever and whenever possible. There in Afghanistan, Clancy creates a character, nicknamed The Archer, to represent other rebels determined to drive out the invading Soviet forces. This man, with little help, uses stinger missiles and concentrates on attacking enemy planes. It seems a David and Goliath situation, but the Archer, like the biblical David, has God/Allah on his side when he undertakes his greatest mission. Unlike David, though, he does not survive that battle.

In another plot, while the Russians are warring with their Afghan neighbors, they are building a huge laser antimissile system, which when perfected will serve as a defense against intercontinental ballistic missile warheads (ICBMs) and satellites. Their facility, with its secret installation, has been code named Bright Star. Not yet a weapon, it is being developed in the area of Dushanbe, high in the mountains belonging to the Soviets, but less than a hundred miles from the border with Afghanistan. The proximity is important to the conclusion of the novel, when the guerrillas destroy much of the site. Thus, seemingly unrelated plots are tied together.

At home, the United States also has a secret facility for research and testing of its own laser project, code named Tea Clipper. They and the Soviets are in a race to complete their laser antiballistic systems, each side concerned about the other's ability to overcome the "enemy's" weaponry. In spite of the fact that the two powers proclaim their interest in peaceful coexistence, they continue to prepare for the possibility of war. Furthermore, each country has set up an elaborate mechanism to gain information about the other's advances with lasers. When the issue is first introduced in the novel, the United States is concerned about the important advances the Russians have made with their laser system, but by the conclusion two important events have occurred. American scientists have moved ahead significantly, and the Russians have been set back by a year or two.

While both East and West work intensely on development of their laser weapons, diplomatic negotiations are taking place to bring about substantial reductions of arms. This is yet another plot. The Russian and American leaders appear to want such changes, but neither country trusts the other, and everything is in a delicate balance. It would take very little to upset the situation; naturally there are numerous individuals and groups working to do just that. There may be a new leader in power at the Kremlin, one the United States believes it can work with in friendship, but his hold is shaky, and Soviet security agencies hope for a misstep. When the various plots in the novel have been resolved, little has changed basically in either the organization of the Committee for State Security (KGB) or the Main Intelligence Organization (GRU), that is, security and intelligence. The chairman of the KGB may have been brought down by American surefootedness, but the agency itself survives.

The major plot and several subplots center on espionage. Spies exist on both sides. Of those, the most important is "the Cardinal," a Russian working for American intelligence. Although he has been providing intelligence to the United States safely for years, an unlucky accident leads to his downfall. At that point the decision must be made whether and how to rescue him. All the agents are skillful in their overt and covert activities and play important roles in the events that take place on both continents, as well as in the cliff-hanging conclusion to the story. As might be expected in this type of fiction, the American side is ultimately faster, sharper, and more skillful in playing the game against Russian intelligence. Various forms of spying that take place in both countries are described, with rapid shifts of scenes from area to area, government facilities, military zones, laboratories, embassies, and even a bath house. The spy sequences are the most exciting parts of the novel, involving drops, cutouts, capture, interrogations, and horrifying modern torture techniques of sensory deprivation.

Clancy brings together the threads and all the plots of the story to achieve a satisfying finale. The Afghan rebels attack and destroy vital parts of the Bright Star facility at Dushanbe. Although their purpose is different from that of the United States, the result gives the latter a stronger position in the arms negotiations. The Tea Clipper project moves ahead after making an important breakthrough, whereas the Russians are set back. The arms talks between the United States and the Soviets survive attempts at dislodging them. The Russian leader, Namarov, whom the United States prefers and supports, is able to maintain his power. The American female spy in the pay of the Russians is ferreted out. And the United States fulfills its moral responsibility to the Cardinal, the Russian spy who has helped it for many years.

With the resolution of the many plots, the requisite chase scenes of an adventure thriller also occur, and because this is a Clancy novel, there is more of everything: chase by car, chase by plane, chase by submarine. With so much action, readers expect casualties on both sides, and the author doesn't let them down. As always, though, most of the good people survive, even if their cover is blown, and their lives change. All ends well. There may be doubt about the United States's relationship with the Russians, but for now the reader can relax, if guardedly.

CHARACTERS

American Heroes

Although this is another in the Jack Ryan "series," Ryan's role is neither as extensive nor as interesting as that of the Cardinal, the Russian spy. For the six months prior to the beginning of the story, Ryan has held a new job in "Arms Control. They want me to coordinate the intelligence side for the negotiations team" (20). Still, he seems much the same as he was in *The Hunt for Red October*. The only noticeable change is in his cars—from the "venerable old Rabbit" to a Jaguar XJS (43). With details of this sort, he begins to look more and more like an adventure figure than a serious professional. Once again he feels uncomfortable that his "education was in history and economics" (119), perhaps because he as Clancy's alter-ego needs to protect himself against a few slips and slides in technology that some critics have referred to.

At the same time that he is self-deprecating, Ryan reviews his accomplishments either externally or internally, from education to wealth to title, Sir John. There are also occasional brief references to his former legendary exploits. When queried about his experiences with Irish terrorists (which occurred in *Patriot Games*), he, though "tired of telling the story," manages to do so anyhow: "You just have to perform, that's all. You either do it right or you lose it." Having said that, he adds a throwaway line, typical of Clancy's style: "If you're lucky, you don't panic until it's over" (150).

Not only is Ryan as heroic as he was in the first novel, but also his activities strongly resemble those earlier ones. Even though this time submarine activities are not his assignment, Ryan, injured once again, helps save the Cardinal as he did Russian Captain Marko Ramius in the first book. He practices subterfuge, plays in the field of an American president and Russian leaders, and at serious risk to his own life preserves everything that is at stake. As one reviewer wrote, "His [Clancy's] hero, Jack Ryan, is maturing nicely into the James Bond of our complicated age" (Books 21).

Another extraordinarily daring American emerges in *The Cardinal of the Kremlin*. He is the mysterious Mr. Clark, who has a small but important role in resolving the spy plots. Although Clark appears and disappears quickly after performing his part of the plan, it seems that the author is creating someone the reader should look for in future novels. (He is next seen in *Clear and Present Danger*.) Even in the somewhat limited description of Clark, enough is given to provide contrast to Ryan. Ryan is very conversational; Clark is laconic; Ryan thinks occasionally about exercise; Clark concentrates on keeping fit. Where Clancy has drawn Ryan as an analytical person trained for intellectual exercise, Clark's persona is that of the man of action. Both men like guns and know how to use them, but Clark really knows weapons, and he carries a gun, not a briefcase like Ryan.

The Cardinal

Even though other people are secretly taken out of Russia, the real object is the rescue of a man not unfamiliar in Clancy's novels. Colonel Mikhail Filitov, affectionately known to friends as Misha, played an important role in *Red October* as a spy for America, but it was barely discussed. In this novel, his part is central, and this time the reader knows him as more than a name. He is the major figure in the major plot. The writer never allows us to forget about him. Clancy's depiction of the old, ailing colonel may be his most successful characterization in all his work. Assuredly, it is in *The Cardinal in the Kremlin*. Admired, as all successful military figures are in Russia, Filitov is different in that he can and does love the Rodina, that is, the homeland, but also can commit treason for what he believes. He resembles Captain Ramius, the Soviet submarine hero of *Red October*, in his duality of feelings.

Clancy shows a lack of inventiveness in the reasons behind Filitov's treason, by making them similar to Ramius's. Both men lost their wives, and Filitov two sons as well. They have nothing left of close human ties. In that, they also replicate the Afghan guerilla, the Archer. All three fight the enemy that deprived them of the personal relationships that made life worthwhile. The root cause of Ramius's and Filitov's defection is the same, the belief that in its inefficiency the system has deceived them. In failing to protect those they loved, Communism has betrayed them. Filitov was a commander of tanks and Ramius of submarines. Yet, each was the very best at his job. Where Ramius defects in taking his vitally important submarine to America, Filitov defects in place. For thirty years he has spied for the United States. Now, in old age, his final act is to gather information about Bright Star, passing it on to the United States through an elaborate system of Russian and American couriers. Though bitterness and disillusionment drive him, he also has a streak of idealism, hoping his actions will help to bring change in a corrupt system.

Because of his status, Filitov, in spite of his age, is allowed to remain an important part of the Soviet government, having access to the newest plans and developments. He commands respect not only because of his military past but also because of his great intelligence. A lonely man, he drinks too much. Yet, in a country known for its problems with alcoholism, he does not impress anyone as a security leak. It isn't the drinking that troubles him or brings about his decisions. Rather, it is all the losses he suffered, not only unnecessarily in his family, but those of friends and comrades in the brutal battles of World War II. At night, alone and drunk on vodka, Filitov sees and hears ghosts out of his past, particularly his old comrade Aleksey Romanov. At the end of his life, having been dramatically rescued from a Soviet prison and flown to the United States, Filitov's last "conversation" is with Romanov. The reader knows then that death is approaching for the old man. Burial is in an unmarked grave at Camp David, the retreat of American presidents. Only the intrusion of some sentimentally jarring notes (plans to name a baby after him) mars the effectiveness of the moving scene at the gravesite of Filitov.

Americans versus Russians

Two parallel figures, from East and West, are involved in their country's efforts to develop effective laser systems. Although they are opposites in most ways, both men are brilliant, loyal products of their country's training. Slight, untidy, unimpressive, and unattractive, Major Alan Gregory looks nothing like the West Point graduate he is. The first impression he makes on anyone is indifferent or even negative. Yet, this theoretical physicist is considered indispensable, a genius who could never be replaced. On the other side is another genius, though he (because he is Russian?) is given a lesser description as "more than just 'clever' " (65). Colonel Gennady Bondarenko, looks impressive, having the appearance of a military man at all times, fit, attractive, crisp, clear, decisive.

Gregory is interested in little but his research and his fiancee, Dr. Candace Long, an expert in adaptive optics, that is, laser mirrors. So engaged are the two of them in their work that even while making love they discuss scientific problems. Bondarenko, also a laser expert, nevertheless is interested and aware of everything in his environment, which he wants to improve. Gregory has acne, probably as the result of eating nothing but junk food, and leaves paper wrappers everywhere. Bondarenko, a highly disciplined career officer, uses both mind and body. He runs, lectures subordinates on healthy living, and also knows his politics. Although he doesn't approve of his country's involvement in Afghanistan, he knows his duty, performing magnificently when Dushanbe is attacked.

Bondarenko has little use for the politicians of Moscow who send young men off to die in warfare. "The politicians never seemed to come close enough to see what they had wrought" (518). Yet, he is also capable of shooting without a second thought an insubordinate officer who will not follow orders during the Afghan attack on Dushanbe. In contrast to Gregory, who is sublimely indifferent to places, cars, food, and rank, Bondarenko is ambitious to be promoted and to make life better for his family. Beneath the exterior differences of the two men, there are many values in common and intelligence that is important to the preservation of their countries. The reader should note, however, that Clancy has given the edge to Gregory by making him a man consumed by science, ambitious only for the advancement of scientific knowledge.

Ambition marks most of the Soviet characters who scheme, lie, torture, and murder as they struggle for power. Those in power will do anything to remain there, and those who seek power will do anything to undermine the others. Some overreach in the competition for control, but others are able to hold on. One of them, Colonel Golovko, will survive some missteps. Perhaps that results in part from his ability to change sides quickly, but more from his attitude toward the bloodless war between East and West: "It was all part of the grand game. The grandest game there was" (33). Golovko will be seen again in a later novel, *The Sum of All Fears*.

Familiar Faces

Just as he will use Golovko in a future plot, Clancy reintroduces characters from one book to another. Apart from his heroes, he assigns different roles and importance to these people. In addition to his two heroes, the American Ryan and the Russian Filitov, and numerous government figures on both sides, Clancy has brought back several others from his first novel. Captain Ramius, now Americanized to Mark Ramsey, has a small but important role aboard the submarine skippered by Captain Mancuso, who will be seen yet again in *The Sum of All Fears*. Mancuso's sonarman, Jones, from *Red October*, though now a civilian, "voluntarily" joins the crew of the *Dallas* for the rescue mission in the Baltic Sea in this novel. Jones also will have a role in the future *Sum*.

STYLE

Clancy follows much of the same pattern in *Cardinal* that he did in earlier works. Frequent shifts of scenes and character provide suspense throughout. Although there is adventure from the beginning, the major plot, with its spy sequences, does not begin to tighten until almost a third of the novel has unfolded. Once that happens, the story and the lesser plots that now become clearly related to the main action become spellbinding. At the same time, even as suspense mounts, Clancy also is successful in creating sympathy for the underdog, the Afghan fighters, who cannot win against the invading Russians. Clancy tells of their suffering, their losses, the harshness of their lives.

Much of the "filler," the non–story line aspects in the novel, has the pleasurable flavor of local color, elements that always appeal to the armchair participant: the subways of Russia, its steam baths, the brutal climate of many of the regions still known then as the Soviet Union, its waterfront and mountain areas. But sometimes the filler becomes tedious, as in long passages about various characters, when the narrator is the author. The reader is told too much and not shown enough. Little dialogue is assigned to characters, and there is too much authorial intrusion meant to influence the audience.

Clancy's quick sense of humor rarely comes through in this novel. Of course, in a work designed to excite, humor would slow down the action, but when he allows his playfulness with language to show, Clancy is fun. For example, when describing a scene in which an American crew has to fly during a Pacific storm, he writes: "What passed for average weather in the Aleutians would close most reputable airports, and what they called bad weather here made the Boeing crew wish for Amtrak" (101). This type of commentary is lighthearted, but much else is heavy-handed.

As all-knowing narrator, the author provides lengthy lessons on technology and physics, sometimes from both the American and Russian side, but now and then a character in the novel takes on the role of instructor. There are also lectures about the Soviet Union, its politics, its economics, its lifestyle. And, to the detriment of the fast pacing required in a thriller, there is again the same type of overkill in the provision of simplistic information most readers know. Ralph Novak, reviewing *Cardinal*, writes that "Clancy . . . has become an explainaholic" and chooses a particularly glaring, yet typical example to make the point. Then, he adds satirically, there is "enough verbal clutter to be a pain in the neck, which is the part of the body connecting the shoulders and the head" (38).

To provide verisimilitude, Clancy goes back to an old technique utilized in the golden age of detective story writers, the 1920s and 1930s. They drew maps of sites, sometimes of real places in which fictional events occurred. On their maps they'd sketch imaginary roads and buildings, even rooms. Clancy does the same. However, he takes the technique a step further in his attempt to make everything seem believable. He first shows an actual aerial map of the mountainous region in which Dushanbe is located and then on the page facing it is his fictive map, which has locations of different structures, towers, bunkers, power lines, and fences. It becomes a place where people live and work in a carefully secured environment.

In most of his novels, Clancy tends to repeat certain expressions, often enough that they become irritating. In earlier books, it was constant reference to one and all Russians as Ivan. Here, it is the term "the old fart," used indiscriminately by Russians and Americans, so that everybody sounds like everyone else. Also, as in other novels, we see the author's proclivity in bringing together machinery and sex. It doesn't matter whether the event takes place in the air or on the ground or what nationality is involved. Machines also seem to bring about the same sexual response from East and West. In *Cardinal*, the sexual simile is even more specific than usual. The Afghan guerilla, the Archer, is shooting a missile at a Russian plane: "As always, it was almost a sexual release when the launcher tube bucked in his hands" (133).

THEMES

The central theme in *Cardinal*, as in much of Clancy's fiction, is the necessity for the strongest possible defense. Enemies are everywhere, and even as they seek accord, they will undermine such actions. Clancy believes that many Americans are naive in trusting the Russians. The novel mirrors history with the struggles between the two world powers to achieve agreements over a wide range of military problems. Because the author does not believe in the reality of the touted successes, his themes focus on the impossibility of accord. He reminds the reader again and again that the Soviets have not changed. Old enemies of the United States, civilian and military, endure as they were. Both the KGB and the GRU remain in place, each vying for supremacy and each a threat to the shaky hold of the Soviet president. In the novel there is no easing of the cold war.

Through several subplots that tell of spies another familiar theme returns. Clancy's Americans are more honorable than his Russians even in the matter of spying. History informs us that spying has been around for hundreds of years in all countries. Clancy, though, stacks the deck in showing a number of Russians, but only one American, willing to betray their country. In reality, there have been and are Americans ready to sell out. One, a navy warrant officer named John Walker, gave vital information to the Soviets for decades. Although the Walker spy scandal occurred before the writing of *Cardinal*, Clancy ignores it completely. His affection for the navy and his confidence in the impregnability of the U.S. undercover system seems to preclude such a possibility. Normal Russians may be spies, but that cannot be the case with normal Americans. In the novel the Russians have good reasons for betrayal, but why would an American turn to spying? Not money. Not power. Not political philosophy. No, here Clancy pushes a homophobic theme. Beatrice Taussig is a lesbian who commits treason because of sexual jealousy. With his avowed bias against homosexuals, Clancy touches a very hot and explosive political issue.

The author's presentation of SDI as a vital defense system supports the central theme, the unchanging need for defense. The SDI was one of the major concerns of the Reagan administration. By making SDI the focus of his primary plot, Clancy can also hammer away at his theme. Where it is historically accurate in the depiction of help given by the United States to the mujahideen, the novel fictionalizes the intervention of the guerrilla fighters in the development of missile systems of the East. In actuality, in 1988, at the end of Ronald Reagan's term, the Soviets began to withdraw from Afghanistan. It was "one of the biggest events of Ronald Reagan's two terms and a turn of seminal significance as well as external policies" (Shultz 1092). However, *Cardinal* does not even begin to suggest its importance.

Rather, Clancy's highlighting of SDI makes it seem far more important than the Afghan War. The fact is that reports vary tremendously on the development of the SDI system and its place in the arms negotiations among great powers. Yet, Clancy makes it a central undertaking of both countries in his version of that historic period. As Clancy historicizes SDI, he has both sides racing for completion of a system whereby they would be able to destroy incoming missiles. The reported facts about the developments appear far different from the novelist's versions. Unlike their fictional SDI counterparts, the real Soviets could not afford such research and development. Although for the United States "the strategic defense initiative . . . proved to be the ultimate bargaining chip" (Shultz 264) in helping negotiations for arms control, but it was no more than that.[1] In actuality, "almost all its original proponents . . . realized that it was too costly and too unreliable ever to be built" (Brinkley 9). But the novelist never even hints at that. The great irony is that he may yet be vindicated and his reputation as a prophet enhanced should SDI research funds be restored and the project bear fruit. There was a post-1994 election proposal from some Republican legislative leaders to revive the defunct SDI project. One Republican budget proposal in 1996 includes funding for SDI; President Clinton is opposed.

ALTERNATE READINGS: HISTORICISM AND THE NEW HISTORICISM

The nineteenth century saw the development of a general critical methodology called historicism. Its central view was that one could understand through literature the history of an era, its social environment, and the characteristics of a group of people. Historic material was considered background to the work of art.

New historicism now takes a totally opposite stand. Politics and art cannot be separated. Most modern historicists insist that art is always an expression of politics. Cognizant of the past, today's historical critic scrutinizes a literary work from a number of perspectives. The text is viewed as an expression of a historic moment in which the writer has constructed or reconstructed some aspects of a time and culture. The critic studies a work partly through "hard" data, that is, facts, evaluating the use to which the author has put them. That evaluation helps form the total judgment of the work. Whereas a traditional historian accepts the "given," the new historicist questions everything. In earlier historicism the literary text is primarily the subject, but contemporary, new historicism is most concerned with "the message" revealed.

To the historical critic (of both persuasions), language is inseparable from history because it situates a culture, an age, a people and their values. The writer's language may be different from the reader's either in time or circumstance. Therefore, the multiple meanings, overt and covert, need to be explored. Language carries a value system that all modern critics, not just the historical, try to penetrate. From one form of criticism to another, linguistic insights vary, but at times they resemble each other.

Always in historicism the author's own life is called into play. Historical critics believe it is essential to know everything about the writer to analyze the influence of his or her experiences on the final literary product. What is "the habit of his mind" (critic Dame Helen Louise Gardner's term) that leads to recurrent themes and ideas? In historicism, there appears to be a meshing of biographical, historical, and psychoanalytic criticism. Further, the historical critic places the individual work within the writer's entire oeuvre and asks: Is the new work similar, different, developmental? Does it seem part of a pattern? To the historical critic, the literary work is part of a lifetime "text," a work ultimately "writ large." That critic also looks at literary influences on the author. Who are the predecessors that led to the form and ideas of the work and who the contemporaries? And, perhaps even more importantly, what is the author's effect on both audience and other writers?

New historicism shares much with the older historicism, but there are important differences. Where older historicists have accepted the written document, the new movement questions interpretations of past events and sometimes even the actuality of such events. (On the matter of interpretation in the new historicism, one might consider the controversies that have arisen over displays shown or planned at the Smithsonian Institute: for example, the decimation of Native Americans as Euroamericans "settled" the West or the atomic bombing of Japan by Americans in 1945. On the question of actuality, there are groups that question the existence of the Holocaust in Europe in the 1930s and 1940s.) The word "revisionist" is frequently applied to these new historicist views. However, the new historicist sometimes responds by labeling traditional historians conservatives dedicated to the status quo.

Although historical critics of the past believed in the potential of objectivity in criticism of texts, the new historicistes believe it cannot be attained. Some modern critics claim to reject value judgments, yet others say that to do so is impossible if there is to be historical awareness. New historicism is suspicious of or skeptical about politics and government, political leaders, and Western culture. For many new historicists the novel is a social text based on other texts, not on empirical knowledge. One of the more important and controversial innovations of the new historicism is a strong scholarly interest in popular culture and cultural studies, in little known or previously unknown works. Where traditional historicists studied the classics, the modern historicist finds significance in other forms of literature.

Tom Clancy's work would not be a subject for traditional historicism because it belongs to the realm of popular culture. Still, one may bring ideas from both historicism and new historicism into an examination of his novels.

With a few exceptions, almost everything in the multiple plots and subplots has some relationship to actual events in the 1980s. The period is that of the historical "glasnost," when the Soviet state was beginning to crack. Clancy's president of the Soviet Union and general secretary of the Communist party, a man named Andrey Narmonov, is modeled after the actual Mikhail Gorbachev in his education, career, and desire to reduce the threat of nuclear warfare. Gorbachev was secretary during the second administration of Ronald Reagan in the United States. Because of Gorbachev's experiences and intelligence, the American "CIA believed [he was] open to influence" (McFarlane 302). That point is made frequently about the fictional Narmonov, whom Clancy makes Gorbachev's double.

Robert McFarlane, Reagan's national security adviser until 1985, is described on the jacket blurb of his book as "the creator of the SDI concept that hastened the downfall of the Soviet Union." George Shultz was secretary of state from 1982 to 1989. Three books—McFarlane's *Special Trust*, Shultz's *Turmoil and Triumph*, and Clancy's *Cardinal of the Kremlin*—concern the same period of time and many of the same events. Yet often the "historic" events reported by McFarlane and Shultz and the fiction of Clancy bear little resemblance to each other. In print, the real government officials frequently criticize each other. Shultz unapologetically speaks of McFarlane's "downbeat attitude" (575) and of his "arrogation of power" (579). McFarlane, less direct but harsher, claims CIA Director William Casey "had a very low regard for Shultz, thinking him to be severely lacking in depth when it came to history and to understanding international politics" (29). As for Clancy, though he mentions neither McFarlane or Shultz by name in his novels, the reader knows his general opinion of people in government. Various characters in his novel jockey for power and control, as did actual players in the Reagan era.

For the reader of these three books the question of the objectivity of historical writers arises. Memoirs and autobiographies were once considered "factual" documents. New historicists regard them as fictionalized, and little more reliable than any other constructed texts and no more believable than novels.

By the time Ronald Reagan left office, George Shultz believed that many positive changes and prospects for change were occurring in the Soviet Union. He worried at the end of Reagan's term that George Bush and his administration might "not understand that the cold war was over" (1138). Whereas Shultz writes of the movement for openness in Reagan's second term, Clancy suggests otherwise. *Cardinal*, like his earlier novels, focuses on hostility and suspicion. Historian Walter Hixson writes that Clancy's novels reflect the Reagan period in "popular perceptions of Soviet behavior and the National Security values" (601). Through his work, the novelist "perpetuate[s] myths about the American past and reinforce[s] the symbols, images, and historical lessons that have dominated the Cold War discourse" (601).

NOTE

1. In their books, Shultz and McFarlane go into lengthy discussion about SDI. For a quick summary, see the *Washington Post*, 12 Dec. 1994: A 21.

7

Clear and Present Danger
(1989)

Publication of his fifth novel made Clancy seem even more prophetic. Dick Williams of the *Atlanta Journal and Constitution* might be speaking for a number of reviewers when he calls the author "clairvoyant." The United States needs him, writes Williams, "not as chronicler but as sooth-sayer" (A23). *Clear and Present Danger* tells a story chillingly close to the reality of the drug industry that has invaded North America. "This is a case of art anticipating life" (Hagman E1). Much information given in the novel came from the author's imagination, but not long after it was published, some "facts" of the story became actuality. Williams suggests that Clancy's careful research may well have led him to discover military plans that had been developed, yet probably not implemented by the government. However, Clancy told Hagman, "The most helpful stuff was really day-to-day news reports" (E2). Still, the number of coincidences is startling.

The venue of *Clear and Present Danger* is different from earlier works, three of which were set primarily in the Soviet Union and one in both the British Isles and the United States. Now the most important setting is the country of Colombia, South America, known to be one of the major sources of drugs coming into North America. Drug cartels in Colombia, rather than the government, are shown as the enemy in a country with which the United States is friendly. The States have declared war on drugs, but such a declaration is difficult if not impossible to implement, given the cordial relations between the two countries. Action has to be taken against the drug lords without aggressive acts against their country. That dilemma is not something Clancy invented.

Several reviewers, though certainly not all, have stated that they think this Clancy's best book after *The Hunt for Red October*. His first novel remains the favorite of many readers. Yet, the author himself now claims to be "embarrassed" by that early novel, "particularly the quality of the writing" (Hagman E2). Are authors the best evaluators of their own work? Not in the view of David Wise. Where Clancy and some others think his writing has become better, Wise says: "For Clancy fans, it probably won't make the least difference that his dialogue has not improved one whit since *The Hunt for Red October*" (9).

Film critics who have read *Clear and Present Danger* often contrast it unfavorably with the movie. Janet Maslin writes that Clancy's "eyeball-glazing prose" has been tamed by the filmmakers, who have a "much more economical style" (C11). The author himself did not attend the world premiere of the movie at the American Film Institute. (One report said he was vacationing, another that he'd not been invited. He has made no effort to disguise his annoyance over the changes from his book.) However, many celebrities were present at the opening of the film, and their statements about the movie are similar to those of book critics. General Colin Powell commented that he always tried "to separate movies and reality." Michael Huffington, a Republican Congressman from California, also "was quick to distinguish movie art from Washington reality," because he didn't find Washington life "that exciting." Democratic Senator Charles Robb of Virginia labeled it escapist fare, even though there were some other people who saw "parallels between the movie plot and . . . Oliver North" (the former marine of Irangate fame whom Clancy supported against Robb in the 1994 senatorial election). The other senator from Virginia, Republican John Warner, thought there might be an "important" lesson in the movie. Warner then spoke of the recent spy scandal that shook the CIA and suggested the film might serve as "a wake-up call" (Donnelly D1). The movie, though much leaner than the novel, carries similar messages in plot and character.

PLOT DEVELOPMENT

Book reviewer James Ward Lee accurately describes the plot as having "more turns and twists than two John Le Carrés and a Robert Ludlum"

(C6). However, as is not the case with some of Clancy's other novels, here it is obvious from the beginning that the parts are all involved with the whole. In spite of the large number of subplots, the reader quickly follows their linkage to the larger story, the drug trafficking between illicit dealers in Colombia and the United States. Actually and fictionally the United States has known for years about the cocaine being brought in from South America on planes and boats belonging to drug cartels. But its ability to control the flow of drugs has been very limited, as has that of the governments of the South and Central American countries. Exploring a "what-if" situation, Clancy's novel describes an attempt to stem the torrent of drugs.

In *Clear and Present Danger* a particularly brutal murder of an American family aboard their yacht sets things in motion. When a Coast Guard ship comes upon the yacht, the discovery leads to information about large money-laundering activities by drug lords. The extent of their penetration into the United States is formidable. Not only do foreign nationals run the drug trade but also numerous Americans are involved in their schemes, their services having been purchased in various ways. The corruption of the drug money touches not only private citizens but even law enforcement employees. Pressure builds both from inside and outside the U.S. government to control if not stop the flow of drugs and destroy the sources of money laundering. As a result, a secret war against a Medellín, Colombia, drug cartel is launched.

The period of time has much to do with the actions of the U.S. president. It is an election year. He and his advisers are concerned about the opposition candidate. Aware of the public anxiety about drugs, they decide that a campaign against drug dealers and their activities will enhance the incumbent's popularity. At first a unit of the air force is secretly designated to shoot down suspicious-looking planes. Their mission is either to destroy the planes or interrogate their pilots about drugs they are carrying and about other drug carriers. As more and more of their illegal planes fail to reach their destinations, the drug lords in Colombia learn of interference with their businesses and bank accounts. The Medellín cartel, infuriated and determined to hit back, makes some hasty and fatal decisions that lead to its own destruction. When it learns that the director of the FBI is being sent by the president to Bogotá, the cartel arranges to have him assassinated. The situation then escalates.

Impetuously, the president, without consulting or notifying Congress, decides to ignore the Colombian government and send specially trained troops into Colombia to destroy drug-processing areas and drug lords.

Initially, the plans are legally questionable. Soon, they are in violation of the U.S. Constitution. The administration finds it impossible to maintain secret operations, although they've even gone so far as to keep their acting deputy director of the CIA, Jack Ryan, from any knowledge of the activities. By the time Ryan learns about the operations in Colombia, everything has begun to sour. With the tacit approval of the president, his special assistant for security affairs has made arrangements with an enemy agent that will sacrifice the covert action American troops. The theory is that the illegal activities will be buried with the soldiers.

Jack Ryan, John Clark, and other brave men step in just in time to prevent the betrayal and abandonment of the soldiers. At great risk to their own lives they are able to save many of them, but before the actions end, a number of people die, both fighters and rescuers. Others get their just rewards. The reprehensible special assistant, who has been bargaining with the enemy, commits suicide. Ryan is promoted from acting deputy director to deputy director. Although members of the Congressional Oversight Committee promise not to reveal their knowledge of the actions the president took in Colombia, it doesn't matter. The president loses the election to the liberal candidate, Jonathan Fowler, and the reader knows there is more trouble ahead for Ryan in the next book.

CHARACTERS

As always in Clancy, the characters are so numerous that it is difficult to remember all of them as they appear and disappear with the rapid changes of settings. Nevertheless, with few exceptions, most fall into Clancy's typical "good guy" and "bad guy" categories. Some of the people are familiar, having appeared in other Clancy novels. In addition to Ryan, from *Patriot Games* there are Bill Shaw and Dan Murray of the FBI, as well as Robby Jackson, Ryan's good friend, the navy pilot who also had a part in *Red October*. Although important to the resolution of the plot lines, they are not action heroes in this novel as are other figures, major and minor.

Minor Heroes

Red Wagener, "the oldest lieutenant-commander in the Coast Guard . . . the Man, the King of Search and Rescue missions" (22) is described in detail throughout the story. A Kansan who did not want to be a wheat farmer, Wegener joined the Coast Guard immediately after high school and rose rapidly in the service as a result of his talents, dependability, and bravery. He is a favorite type of Clancy hero: "It was evident that when a tough job had to be done, his name was the one that came up first" (23). Both loved and admired by his ferociously loyal crew, Wegener knows they will do anything he asks of them. Wegener, his men, and his boat *Panache* provide a nice kind of structural circle to the novel. At the beginning, they encounter the yacht belonging to the people who have been murdered by members of the drug ring. At the end, Wegener and the crew of the *Panache* help in the rescue of American troops from Colombia.

Another minor, yet important heroic figure, is Carlos Larson, who lives and works in Colombia. Although he is actually an undercover CIA agent, his work as a pilot and flying instructor has led to his acquaintance with members of the Medellín cartel. An important source of information about the movement of drugs to the United States, Larson also risks his life again and again in the attempts to destroy the cartel and to save the covert American troops from annihilation when their cover is blown. Larson is a very attractive character, young, romantic, daring, an eye-catching contrast to the military figures. Nevertheless, though Larson is a freelancer with a devil-may-care attitude, he is no more reckless than the older air force colonel, Paul Johns, who is willing to violate orders to save the troops.

Johns's close friend, Master Sergeant Buck Zimmer, loses his life during the rescue effort. Although Zimmer is meant to be yet another example of a sacrificial hero, the reader remembers him because of his wife, an Asian refugee, and their large family. Mrs. Zimmer's background gives Clancy a way to voice his position about the Vietnam War, and Zimmer's death provides Jack Ryan the opportunity to show his feelings and his generous heart. In a death scene befitting the sentiment of a nineteenth-century Victorian novel, Ryan promises the dying man to send his children through college.

Major Heroes

Three very distinct types of men, all memorable, are central to the novel. Staff Sergeant Domingo (Ding) Chavez is new to the Clancy novels but is seen again in the next one. John Clark, who had a miniscule part in *Patriot Games* and a limited role in *Cardinal,* now becomes a major player. And, as in six of Clancy's novels, Jack Ryan is present.

Chavez represents Clancy's beliefs in what military service can do for poor, underprivileged, uneducated young people when they are determined to improve their lot in life. Before enlisting in the army, Chavez had been a gang member with nothing to look forward to except the possibility of death in gang warfare. In the service he overcomes his illiteracy and masters every type of training the army puts him through, so that he becomes a combat leader in the light infantry. Small, lean, and quick, Chavez is an ideal, and idealized, soldier. Proud of what he has become, he feels forever indebted to the army. Nothing that is asked of him is too much. He typically voices the same battle cry to any officer who questions his ability to perform death-defying acts: "We own the night" (50) proclaims Chavez, his battle cry symbolizing his resolute personality.

Sent to Colombia with other specially trained young Spanish-speaking men, he is outstandingly brave and resourceful. Motivated by a high sense of duty to the country he loves, even when he wonders about the wisdom or value of an operation or an order, he performs superbly. Chavez could well serve as a legend for a recruiting office. So superior is his performance in battle and in helping to save the remnants of his group after they have been betrayed and abandoned that he catches the attention of CIA agent John Clark, himself a legendary figure of unqualified bravery.

Clark is a chameleon. Few people really know him or his history. (We learn more about him in a later book, *Without Remorse.*) Even the name Clark is not real. His background is vague, but it has been violent. Clark has two lives, one as a family man with wife and daughters, the other as an expert in "special, short, dangerous jobs" (45). Like a one-man army, Clark himself is dangerous not only to the enemy but also to those he regards as betrayers, as moral cowards. Not a man to toy with, he keeps his promises.

Fortunately, Clark is one of "our" people. He is a dangerous and ruthless adversary, yet attractively so as such figures are. "On instinct, most men watched their behavior around Mr. Clark. John Clark did not have horns and hooves, but it seldom took more than a single glance to know that he was not to be trifled with, either" (282). Is Clark still another representative character of Clancy's "dark" side as some critics have suggested? The first three letters—C-l-a—of his name lend some credence to the idea that the author identifies with him.

Again, as in *The Cardinal of the Kremlin*, the reader is aware of the strong contrasts between Clark and Jack Ryan. Although Clancy would not intentionally draw Ryan as a weaker figure than Clark, that impression lingers in the first part of the novel. Ryan seems to have to work himself up to action, but Clark never. Ryan is kept ignorant of the activities in Colombia. Clark is a participant. Ryan has suspicions but doesn't force them out into the open until his friend Robby Jackson comes to him with information he can't ignore.

Ryan has been kept out of the inner circle of knowledge by several officials. Among them is CIA Deputy Director (Operations) Robert Ritter who hasn't much confidence in Ryan at first. Then, in a now conventional abrupt about-face that the author uses with Ryan, Ritter changes his mind because of his respect for Ryan. When Ryan is promoted to "one of the premier intelligence posts in the world" (215) Ritter is approving. But Ryan himself seems hesitant about his ability. From episode to episode he manages to keep his temper until he is confronted by the ultraliberal "assistant adviser for foreign policy" of presidential candidate Fowler. When she, Elizabeth Elliot, makes an insinuating remark, he storms at her: "I have two children and a wife, who also graduated Bennington.... I'm not James Bond and I don't fool around" (445). Clancy explains Ryan's explosion by noting that he's had a "long day," that he was "suffering jetlag." Further, "nobody had ever pushed Ryan's buttons that hard before" (447). Both the outburst and the author's defense of Ryan might surprise readers. Ryan has endured many dangerous events—injuries, cold war confrontations, arrest, accidents, and threats on his and his family's lives. One has to wonder what is at issue when he finds a hostile woman more threatening than all of those.

Not long after that confrontation, Ryan once again hears the call to action. With that he is ready to take on everything and everyone to right the wrongs that have been done. He defies his superiors, including the president, and we find him very much like James Bond, Superman, or Batman; he joins forces with Clark and other rebels to save the remnant of the combat troops that have been abandoned and betrayed by the administration.

Villains: Ours

While one expects the enemy to be evil, it is a shock to learn that equally dangerous people are part of the government. In this novel Vice

Admiral James Cutter is such a person. Serving as national security adviser, Cutter is a major influence on the president. Always with an eye on his own position and future, Cutter plays a game intended to promote his welfare. Clancy points to Cutter's arrogance with this kind of commentary: "Cutter was past caring what little people thought of him" (14).[1] He comes from an old wealthy Yankee family and has had all the required commands to move up the ladder. But Ryan wonders if Cutter became NSA adviser because he "polished up the knocker faithfully." Because of his dislike, Ryan is convinced "the three-star Admiral was in over his head, but had not the sense to realize it" (117).

Cutter is adept at shifting responsibility to others. If things go well, he gets the credit; if badly, the blame settles elsewhere. His activities in promoting the covert war and then attempting to end it through betrayal of the troops lead to his downfall. Believing himself more clever than all the CIA, FBI, and the military, he is unable to imagine that someone like John Clark, a man of lesser education, power, and position, can outmaneuver him. Because such characters as Clark and Cutter are kin to those in medieval morality plays, representing struggles between good and evil, in the end, evil must be destroyed. Clark wins, and Cutter dies.

Villains: Theirs

Two figures are vital in the cartel cause. One, Ernesto Escobedo, is a leading member of the Medellín group. Monstrous in his pursuit of power, a man without any human feelings, Escobedo, who never contemplates pity or kindness, seems more evil than Felix Cortez, whom he employs. He is entirely a man of the flesh, whereas Cortez is highly disciplined and cunning. Clancy has drawn Cortez as more complex than Escobedo. There are multiple layers to his character. Although Cortez does terrible things, he is capable of regretting them. Cortez reminds us of an Iago figure, one of William Shakespeare's smiling villains who will betray both men and women to gain his own ends. Yet, even as Cortez commits cruel or violent acts, he takes a brief moment to clear the conscience that pricks him. His smiling mask conceals the jealousy, rancor, ambition, and arrogance that drive him. These are the same qualities inherent in the famous villains of literature. He catches the interest of the reader as no flatly evil character can. And, ultimately, justice is meted out to him like the villains of old.

Women

A few women are part of the story, but only one has a significant role in the plot line. Moira Wolfe, secretary to the director of the FBI, Emil Jacobs, inadvertently provides information that leads to his death. Seduced by Felix Cortez, Moira, simple soul that she is, hasn't a clue to his motivation. If it were not for Moira's embarrassing naiveté and lines of dialogue, the reader would hardly remember her. But her tearful gratitude at sexual fulfillment and her sparkling eyes that later inform co-workers about it remind the reader of the author's failure to create interesting or realistic female characters.

Clancy is even less successful with his brief introduction to Elizabeth Elliot, the woman who "pushes" Ryan's "buttons." Where Moira Wolfe is sweet and not too bright, Elizabeth Elliot is bitchy and devious. Although she is the assistant to Jonathan Fowler, the aspiring candidate for the presidency, there is no clear reason for Elliot's appearance in this story. Clancy seems to be laying some groundwork for the novel that follows. In *The Sum of All Fears* Elizabeth Elliot will be seen as both adviser and mistress to President Fowler.

STYLE

Clancy's style is unchanged from his earlier works. As always, he expands the work with much technical information: planes, bombs, coded disks, encrypted messages, satellite dishes, cellular phones, specially trained troops. He also provides instruction on the making of jailhouse weapons and ways to save a suicide. Sometimes he forgets he has used some of the technical information in an earlier book. In *Clear and Present Danger* we are told much the same thing about protective windows in cars as we were in *Patriot Games*. However, descriptions of settings in the you-are-there mode are again intriguing and exciting. The author may not have been to Colombia, but he puts the reader in the mountains and jungles of that country, amid the rain, heat, and mosquitoes.

Dialogue remains weak. Too often it is a case of one size fitting all. Clancy rarely uses direct dialogue to reveal character but provides information either as omniscient author or in a very simple form of interior commentary: "Ryan thought." He continues to employ scatological language, such as the familiar "old fart" and the more recent "shit happens." At the opposite end of the language scale, he utilizes lines that sound like an elegant translation from Spanish or have the effect of reading Hemingway when he is attempting to capture the flavor of Spanish: "He had pleased her greatly" (188).

THEME

A central theme about the military runs through Clancy's books. It is that fighting men and women in the various branches of service are almost invariably heroic, selfless, and dedicated people. All too often government betrays them for strategic or political reasons. Clancy implants the idea from the beginning, on his acknowledgments page. After thanking a number of people, mostly military, Clancy says, "Would that America served you as faithfully as you serve her."

In the story that follows, that theme is predominant. It supports the view that the true heroes are the men on the front line. They are the "grunts," the combat soldiers, sailors, fliers who die for their country. Yet the government they serve doesn't place much value on their lives, says Clancy through Ryan. They follow orders, believing that what they do is important. "The oath our people take when they put on the uniform requires them to bear 'true faith and allegiance' to their country. Isn't it written down somewhere that the country owes them the same thing?" (652–653). The story he has told is that the country, the administration, the Congress, all who control the destiny of ordinary soldiers, betray them.

ALTERNATE READING: MASS CULTURE THEORY

Most detective, suspense, and thriller books may be analyzed under the umbrella of mass culture theory. These works, by and large, *are* mass culture and are easily differentiated from high or elite art. Much mass culture theory is opposed to popular media of all types: entertainment literature, television, films, painting, and music. These are seen as instruments leading to the decay of a society because, says the theorist, vital issues are treated simplistically, generally, and superficially. The audience is soothed, amused, and reassured but never challenged intellectually. Often a reviewer consciously or unconsciously writes a piece that has been influenced by theories of mass culture. Thus, the review might focus on the negative effect of *Oprah* in television, on the simplistic "feel-good" qualities of the movie *Forrest Gump,* or the sterility of Andy Warhol paintings, or on the destructive element of rock music.

The particular newspaper, magazine, or journal, as well as editors' choices of reviewers, frequently indicates the theoretical orientation of the article. Popular fiction often is treated less favorably in eminent papers and journals than in less elite publications. The material and audience are different as well.[2] Although unfavorable reviews rarely keep large numbers of the public from reading popular fiction, even the most successful writer wants approbation. Clancy is a prime example. He attacks reviewers and literary critics who write disparagingly of both the style and contents of his books.

Mass culture theory usually holds the view that a superior culture exists, that is, a "high" culture. Sometimes a work under review is measured according to that view. The theorists see popular material as destructive to a superior level of civilization or high culture. Large numbers of people are deluded by mass culture, which is actually reactionary, say these theorists. They believe that the much valued industrialization since the last century has produced a mechanized society. This, in its turn has created a violence-filled world and a roboticized population exploited by commercialization. Technology, which should improve the lives of people educationally, economically, and culturally, is controlled by a power structure. Various names are given to this: the "establishment," the government, the "military-industrial complex" (Brantlinger 230). Mass culture theorists argue that technology has done as much harm— or more—than good. That point is supported by a review of historic events in the twentieth century. The theorists hold that mass cultural media (television, films, popular literature) support the status quo and destroy motivation for change. These force out "high," or intellectual culture through various means, but primarily economic ones.[3]

Clear and Present Danger, like all of Clancy's novels, may be seen through the lens of mass culture theory. The writer's ideas, attitudes, likes, and dislikes ride on the surface of the novels. He lets the audience know of his scorn for Congress—the members leak information. He shows his irritation with people on welfare and the system that permits it—people living on food stamps driving up to stores in cars. He reveals his preference for cartels over Marxist groups—better to kill the latter than the former. Once again he makes known his aversion to gays— along with his prescription of prison sodomy as fit punishment for terrorists or those who commit treason. He emphasizes his view that the

United States should have remained in Vietnam and states that in its withdrawal before destroying the enemy, this country betrayed the Vietnamese people.

People "on top," the president and his advisers, the new "corporate Navy" (Clancy's term), career officers ambitious only for themselves, and some intelligence directors often take a cold view of the price paid for actions they've ordered. In this novel, few pay attention to the deaths of Colombian civilians and American soldiers. "That's a cost of doing business, sir," says the president's special assistant for National Security Affairs (395). Political gain is uppermost in their minds. Venality is all, and the message conveyed through the media of books and film is that those at the top are not to be trusted.

Jack Ryan lectures the president, telling him "in breaking the rules, sir, you took a national-security issue and made it into a political one" (651). Ryan's valor has been reinforced by the deathbed lecture of his friend and mentor the deputy director of CIA intelligence. He says to Jack: "Politics? All that shit?" What matters are "ideas," "principles," and "words." "Your word is who you are" (491–492). The suggestion is that only certain types of people are to be trusted, types singled out and respected by Ryan and the author.

Ryan is always wary of politics and politicans, unless they are pro-military. Among the politically oriented civilians he works with, he is shown to be more high-minded than they are. His faith is with the military and intelligence agents, not with elected officials. The military will face any hardship sent them and be victorious if they are not undermined at home. These ideas have been labeled "Ollie North fantasies" by Shuger, who claims that they are reassuring to most readers. They probably have not been in the military or had very limited experience, so that they believe the message that all is well, that "everything is under control. Don't worry" (18).

According to mass culture theory, this type of communication is dangerous for readers because it masks reality. Subliminal messages register about superiority and invincibility. The audience is being told it is better than politics and politicians. Further, if one's ideas, principles, and words are right (the language used by Ryan's mentor), that individual may take the law into his or her own hands. Why not? The message is carried and made stronger with each successive book in the person of Jack Ryan and John Clark.

Shuger warns that a message of superiority and invincibility is most dangerous for the "military men and political leaders [who] unflinchingly accept the message too, even though it makes about as much sense for the Pentagon to consult Tom Clancy as it does for the Supreme Court to consult the producer of 'L.A. Law' " (18). Mass culture theorists would agree.

NOTES

1. The term "little people," with the emphasis on "little," foredates statements made by New York hotel owner Leona Helmsley that brought an angry reaction from the public.

2. Clancy's work is reviewed in magazines like *Time* and *Newsweek* but not in the *New York Review of Books* or the *Times Literary Supplement* (London).

3. A useful example of this is the ongoing battle over the role of public broadcasting, which has been labeled "elitist" by some members of government who have the economic power to support or destroy it.

8

The Sum of All Fears
(1991)

If Clancy were to read all the reviews of his sixth novel, would he, any more than the reader, be able to sort out any general agreement among the critics? Ted Williamson of the *Detroit News and Free Press*, calls it "a very uneven book" with a "silly conclusion" (Q7). Many label it overlong. After all it is almost 800 pages. Reviewers compare it unfavorably to Clancy's early work, *The Hunt for Red October*, which was half the length and had tighter plotting. Some would have cut this novel by 150 pages, some by 200. However, most reviewers say in spite of the length, the riproaring, nail-biting conclusion is worth the slow-moving descriptions used to get there. Although only a few dedicated reviewers call it his best work—Howard Kaplan of the *Denver Post*, for example—Clancy himself told an interviewer "It's the best writing I've done. And it's a subject that's important" ("The Write Stuff":16). The reader who asks what makes the subject matter of this novel any more important than the earlier ones might find the answer in the plot and in the message conveyed by it.

PLOT DEVELOPMENT

A plan to end hostilities in the Middle East, proposed by but not credited to Jack Ryan, is agreed to by Israelis, Arabs, Americans, Russians, and various other concerned nations. The first significant hope for peace between Israel and her neighbors comes with a treaty signed at the Vatican. However, this movement toward peace does not suit anti-Israel factions. One of them, an Arab terrorist group, through violent action, attempts to counter the accord. So successful are these terrorists in their activities, they almost bring about a third world war.

Fortuitously for the Arab terrorists, they come upon the remnants of an atomic bomb. Drawing on members of other terrorist and intelligence groups, who in turn recruit trained scientists and workers, they form a team to build a workable bomb. With its completion the terrorists transport their newly made hydrogen bomb to a stadium in Denver, where the NFL Super Bowl game is scheduled. The terrorists believe the explosion will be viewed as a Russian attack on America. If so, retaliation will follow, and Israel will then be vulnerable because American interest will have shifted to other parts of the world. Although the bomb does kill massive numbers of Americans, including both the secretary of state and secretary of defense, its effect is not as far reaching as the terrorists hoped. Still, for a short period of time the relationship between the United States and Russia is heated and dangerous. War seems unavoidable.

When the U.S. president, Jonathan Fowler, learns that Iran has bankrolled the entire terrorist operation, he wants to bomb the Iranian city Qum. Jack Ryan, now director of the CIA (Intelligence), intervenes, preventing the issuance of an order to attack Iran and the certainty of war. His actions bring on a crisis that forces the president to resign. At the last moment, all the disparate parts of the plot come together. Ryan saves the day, not to say world peace.

Other Plots

James Ward Lee calls the multiple subplots such "a tangled web" that only Jack Ryan can "untangle" everything (C5). The reader, lacking the talents of Jack Ryan, has to struggle to keep track of all that is happening and also to find the thread of relationships to the major plot.

Among the many lesser plots is the ongoing struggle for power in Russia, reported to Washington by a spy who misleads the U.S. administration. At the same time, problems are reported aboard an American submarine with "an ambitious, Queeg-like captain" (Kaplan 2). Again, as in several earlier books, submarines are tracked by both Americans and Soviets. Another subplot tells the story of a few criminal American Indians, one of whom becomes a member of the Mideast terrorist group. We also learn of the inadequacy of the American president to deal with major problems. The rise to power of the president's mistress, Elizabeth Elliot, highlights his weaknesses. Her enmity toward Jack Ryan brings on a different kind of war, which becomes sordid, as she attempts to force his dismissal or resignation. Troubles at work lead to problems in Ryan's marriage: fatigue, liquor, and impotency.

CHARACTERS

Old Familiars

Americans and Russians from earlier books are brought back in large numbers. Most of them are minor, even insignificant figures, who appear briefly and then are dropped from the story. Among the Americans is history professor Father Riley, the brilliant Jesuit from Georgetown University. First seen in *Patriot Games*, Father Riley here serves as the initiating force between the United States and the Vatican to bring about a peace treaty in the Middle East. Once that is accomplished, Riley plays no further role in the story. In an effort to obtain verisimilitude, Clancy shows all the characters as older than in his earlier novels and most of them further advanced on the career ladder. From *The Hunt for Red October*, *Patriot Games*, and *Clear and Present Danger* there is Robby Jackson, Ryan's old friend, now commander of an air group (CAG). He is aboard the *Theodore Roosevelt*, a nuclear-aircraft carrier and flagship in the Mediterranean Ocean. Jackson gets into some of the military action during a short and dangerous air carrier confrontation between the United States and Russia. Former Submarine Commander Bart Mancuso, now a captain designated to be a rear admiral, also shows up in a few scenes. Readers will remember him for his heroic leadership in *Red October* and *The Cardinal in the Kremlin*. As with Jackson, Mancuso's skills have been recognized, so that he now leads a Pacific Fleet squadron. Following the pattern of earlier novels, he turns again for help to his former sonarman, the talented Ron Jones, who has left the navy, earned a doctorate, and occasionally serves as a civilian consultant.

Another familiar minor figure is William Shaw, first introduced in *Patriot Games* and later in *Clear* as a member of the FBI. Shaw, too, has moved up professionally, to become the director of his agency. Dan Murray, his friend and associate, also seen in the earlier books, started as a special agent and now is deputy director of the FBI. Although Shaw and Murray are not major players in *Sum*, they have roles that are significant in the working out of the major plot. From the other intelligence agency, the CIA, Mary Pat Foley, last seen in *Cardinal*, is reintroduced. Mary Pat, pregnant once again, is now back in Washington working for the agency. A feisty and interesting character in the earlier book, she is less so here, even though she remains part of the spy network, having recruited another Russian spy. That person, Oleg Kadishev, code named Spinnaker, turns out to be a disaster because the information he provides leads the United States and Russia to the brink of a nuclear war.

A new member of the CIA, Ding Chavez, was one of the major military heroes of *Clear*. At the conclusion of that book, the awesome John Clark recruited him, and he has become Clark's assistant, learning the "trade" from him. His serious and sturdy nature is emphasized more than his physical exploits. Intent on bettering himself, he takes courses at night at George Mason University. Chavez is insignificant in this novel, but also Clark's part is smaller. Even more disappointing to the reader is Clark's dullness, compared to his swashbuckling role in *Clear*. A reader unfamiliar with the earlier book might not know quite what to make of Clark now. As a man of all trades Clark is a diminished figure. Only in the last part of *Sum* does he perform the daring actions we have come to expect of him.

Clark: The Dark Hero as Busybody

Serving as a general factotum, Clark plays just about every role except baby-sitter for the Ryan family and friends. His major function in *Sum* is as combination chauffeur and bodyguard for Jack Ryan. Accustomed to a more adventurous life, Clark seems at times to chafe at the responsibility of guarding Ryan. When protecting himself, he had choices and a complete freedom of movement. Now, self-protection is no longer his central concern. Rather, he appears more like a cop on the beat than a deadly and dangerous opponent. In one episode (that has little point in the scheme of the novel) he and Chavez "set things right" (47) with a gang that has been threatening to Carol Zimmer, the wife of Ryan's late friend.

Clark generally waits to be asked for his views. However, when Ryan talks with him about the situations in the Middle East, Clark expresses his ideas about the Saudis and Israelis. He likes both, though they are different from Americans. Voicing some of Clancy's thoughts, Clark is sympathetic to the Israelis because of their suffering during the Nazi era. Like Clancy, Clark wonders why America did not come to the rescue of the millions of Jews.[1] Fundamentally a man of action, Clark seems to want to right whatever wrongs he finds. In this novel, he has limited opportunity to do so, and it seems wasteful of the author not to use Clark more. Only rarely do we catch a glimpse of the great adventurer we've seen before. Late in the novel Clark reveals his daring and more of his skills when he "bugs" the plane of the Japanese prime minister, thus providing secret information for Ryan and the CIA. Clark also has a prominent part in the capture of the Arab terrorists who built and planted the hydrogen bomb in Colorado.

At other times in this novel, Clark seems more the "Big Daddy" or life counselor than death-defying adventurer, and such roles waste him. Without being queried, he frequently voices his opinion about Ryan's overworked and exhausted appearance. Using strong language, he attempts to shock Ryan into awareness of his health. However, he never misses the chance to praise Ryan to others, even though he isn't a talkative man. Thus, when he learns that Ryan's marriage is in trouble, Clark takes it upon himself to tell Cathy Ryan how wonderful her husband is, how proper, upright, generous, and saintly. Clark carries this interference further. In a calculated move, he gives top secret information to a reporter (with the admonition that he may never use it). In exchange the reporter provides names of people who are smearing Ryan publicly and privately, causing devastating effect on his personal and professional life. When Clark learns all, he passes on the knowledge to Ryan's wife. It works wonders for the marriage. Cathy Ryan goes on the offensive, and the marital rift is healed, thanks to Clark.

Ryan: Hero under Stress

When first seen in *Sum*, Jack Ryan is doing well in his new job, appreciated by many of the people around him. But unexpected events change that, and everything begins to go sour for him. Ryan is prickly because he is not given credit for the work he's done. When the national security adviser to the president dies only to be replaced by Ryan's avowed enemy, Elizabeth Elliot, it seems as if an internecine war is underway. He gets little or no support for his recommendations or decisions. Worse, he is constantly undermined by Dr. Elliot. Tired all the time, depressed by his lack of energy and inability to sleep, he begins to drink more and more. He seems less and less able to cope with daily existence.

Clancy once again, as in earlier books, provides a thorough review of Ryan's impressive background, his education, jobs, wealth, and generosity. To the reader, however, Ryan too often appears indecisive, petty, irascible, and self-pitying. His anger focuses on Elizabeth Elliot, rather than on his inability to solve his problems in his office and in his bedroom. Although he periodically reviews his past achievements and present qualifications for his job, he seems unconvincing. He confides to his old friend the prince of Wales that he's under stress and drinking too much but won't take the prince's advice to give up the work he's doing. The prince also warns him about pride. Ryan denies it, saying the administration needs him: "I wish they didn't, but they do." Contrasting their two situations, he says the prince has no option because of his birth, but that he, Ryan, is "just as stuck" with his job "because I'm the guy best able to do it" (432–433).

The author appears to waffle on the political and philosophical views his hero holds. Early in the novel, Ryan is said to have seen himself "as a servant, not a master, an implementer of policy" (97). Somewhere that view gets lost. Ryan supplants the president twice. Although President Fowler is said to be out of control, it seems at the very least equally true of Ryan. It is startling and unacceptable to read someone's flattering thought about Ryan: "He envied Ryan's ability to control himself" (750). "Control" hardly seems the appropriate word to describe Ryan's demeanor as the action heats up. For much of the story Ryan does little but brood about his inability to act. Then it is as if a bell has rung and the fighter comes out ready to do battle, to take over, to issue orders. In the final battle between Ryan and Fowler, Ryan tells people to "ignore" the president, and he himself takes command.

Jabbing "a finger into the President's chest," Ryan explodes, saying to him: "You're the one who fucked up! You're the one who took us to the edge" (783). The reader can almost hear the cheers of the audience—in a future movie?—as Ryan saves both the country and the world from certain doom. The president, forced to resign in disgrace, has been defeated by Jack Ryan. Ryan's material reward comes later in the form of a 300-year-old sword awarded to him by Prince Ali of Saudi Arabia. The magnificent sheath and handle are made of gold, ivory, and jewels. It was "manifestly the weapon of a king." The suggestion cannot be overlooked that Ryan be considered a king of kings. The sword will always be a reminder for him of "what it and he had done" (796). With this conclusion, the reader might well wonder what has happened to the humorous, self-deprecating Ryan of *Red October*.

STYLE

This is a novel which provides details of many kinds, some interesting, some tedious. History lessons given by the author explain the religious problems and wars of the Middle East, the Druse people, the changes in modern Russia, the function of the American vice-presidency. The medical facts of a stroke are described, as are war games, the interior of a presidential plane, the workings of sonar, the elements of plutonium and tritium. There are lectures on arms reduction, communications systems, and once more—submarines. In that same vein, references to the *Red October*, the submarine of the author's first novel, are scattered throughout. Football players, styles, and records, even the scores are discussed. While the importance of football to the plot becomes clear late in the novel, the details about it do nothing but slow down the suspense as do many of the other discussions and descriptions.

Clancy follows the conventions of mystery writing by including much local color in *Sum*. Various places abroad and at home are real and often familiar to readers. A native and resident of Maryland himself, Clancy locates many fictional activities in the greater metropolitan Washington area. Ryan and Clark drive the local expressways and read the *Washington Post*. Fort Meade and Fort Ritchie, military bases in the Maryland district, are the settings of some episodes, as is the presidential retreat, Camp David (which Clancy has also shown in other novels.)

Language here resembles that of earlier books, and, as before, characters from different professions and of different gender frequently sound the same. One of Clancy's favorite expressions, "old fart," is voiced by FBI men Shaw and Murray, and also by Elizabeth Elliot. However, it is meant to be funny when the men say it, but nasty when the woman uses it; the men laugh, and she snarls. The effect, though, raises a question about language used by men and women: Does Clancy give masculine sounding thoughts and words to Dr. Elliot to make her appear "unfeminine" or vulgar? He describes her as thinking of one of her colleagues as an "asshole" who hasn't enough sense to avoid "shtuping" one of his students (89). As she follows up the thought, she phones the president to report the offense, hoping he isn't "on the crapper" (90). Because Clancy doesn't have other women speak that way, the reader questions whether this language is coded. Does it hold special meaning for the writer and some readers?

Another jarring linguistic note appears in the novel with the nickname given to Robby Jackson, an African American. "Spade," is painted on Jackson's plane so that people know it is "the CAG's bird" (304). Jackson also refers to himself as Spade when identifying himself to his men in flying. Again, one must wonder whether this is Clancy being humorous or tweaking the sensitivities of the reader by being the opposite of politically correct. Whatever the purpose, it does misfire.

THEMES

Patrick O'Brian writes that *The Sum of All Fears,* which "is about four times the length of the usual novel," also deals with at least four times the usual number of themes (X1). In spite of the large number, the major themes are substantial, touching on most of the issues of our lives, of war and peace, of politics, of education, of public and private morality. Clancy's story warns not only of the possibility of terrorist infiltration, but also of the dangers of nuclear war.[2] There is danger from within and without. The themes meld in emphasizing the need to guard against complacency. When the "wrong" people control government, the entire globe is in danger. A weak president and a liberal Congress will betray and destroy military and civilian alike. Clancy takes swipes at Congress, his favorite whipping boy for many things, but particularly what he sees as its lack of understanding about the defense of the United States.

A lesser group of themes develops the idea that various types of liberalism lead to problems large and small. Clancy's general dislike of liberalism comes through in a declaration of the value of hard punishment for criminals, briefly telling of two young Sioux arrested for robbery. He describes the judge as having "more compassion than perception" (53), someone who arranges for counseling rather than applying a strict code of discipline. Instead of learning that criminal acts result in harsh penalties, the two thieves are instructed to give up theft in order to develop a better self-image. All they gain from the counseling is a sense of wonder "how the Sioux Nation had ever allowed itself to be overrun by white idiots." They return to their former life, having "learned to plan their crimes more carefully" (53). Clancy blames many of the problems of Indians on the American Indian Movement, noting scornfully that they have simplified everything to vilification of white men. Nevertheless, he does suggest there are serious root causes as well for Indian problems, such as the inadequate school programs. The problem of poor schools is a theme Clancy develops in essays as well as fiction.

Flaunting educational background is good if connected to characters the author likes. Thus, praise is given to an Asian mother who is "like most Asians . . . in her reverence for learning" (215). Further, when Ryan quotes a line from T. S. Eliot's play *Murder in the Cathedral*, that is all right. However, the old anger toward some other American poets surfaces again. This time the criticism is not from Ryan but a Marine officer who deals in encrypted messages. He sends his Russian counterpart lines from Emily Dickinson, "a morbid bitch, always talking about death and stuff. No, better yet—Edgar Allan Poe. They really like him over there" (182). That liking means a demerit for the Russians. If they enjoy Poe or Dickinson, they can't have taste or judgment. Although the Russians are not central in this novel, the author can't resist a swipe at them.

The author also reveals a stern morality that appears as antiliberalism. Morality as a theme surfaces in unrelated comments and episodes throughout the novel, but they all add up to a schema for proper living. Driving and drinking are not permitted, as Cathy Ryan reminds her husband at a White House party. She has champagne, while he meekly takes Perrier. Scattered again through the novel are several "humorous" references to gays, of whom he disapproves. Clancy also seems to find it necessary to note the marital status of various characters, even if they are unnamed and never to be seen again. Sexual propriety and impropriety often are commented on. Sex is permitted between divorced or widowed people, the president and his mistress, for example. Marital sex has greater limitations. Ryan is shown in a love scene "with his wife . . . expressly for the purpose of making babies" (Menand 92). Single men also may have sex. In a passing scene, two sailors are talking about their desire to get "laid." The author tells the reader their longings are acceptable, as he ends their brief discussion with this sentence: "Both men were single" (444).

No Clancy novel exists without some military theme. Here Clancy's attitudes about the Vietnam War are expressed bluntly. He uses the word "betrayal" to describe the American pullout. He has various characters (no matter what importance they have to the plot) refer to promises made and broken in Vietnam. It is one of Clancy's passions. The theme takes on heightened significance when we learn that the novelist's next book has Vietnam as part of the major plot.

ALTERNATE READING: READER-RESPONSE CRITICISM—RHETORIC AND ITS FUNCTION

The focus of reader-response criticism is on the influence or effect of the text on the reader. Where many earlier forms of literary theory focused on the idea of an objective text, reader-response criticism rejects that concept, claiming that the text is subjective because each reader interprets it differently.

Some critics separate different kinds of readers into categories. One is the actual reader, the person who buys or borrows and reads the book. Another is the conceived reader, the person the author *thinks* is the audience and whom he or she endows with certain specific characteristics. Then there is the idealized or "model" reader, someone able to understand every implication or suggestion, the language, knowledge, and expectations of the author. The fact that such a reader is nonexistent, that there really is no "model reader," does not alter the author's conception of such a person. Whatever type of reader, recognition of the reader as a participant or influence on a text changes the perspective of both the writer and the critic.

One interpretation of reader response holds that the meaning of a book is shaped for the reader by the conventions, that is, the traditions of literature, society, and culture at a particular time. Other critics theorize that readers respond to texts as to the events in their lives, so that they transfer the personal into the general. Meaning, then, is understood through individual experience. As a result, the reader plays a role in creating textual meaning out of his or her own experiences. However, the reader does not have quite as much free choice as that statement suggests. The text must support the argument. Although many possible interpretations exist, there are limits.

Readers need to be cautious in interpreting a writer's intentions. The writer's text or the critic's interpretation may be politically motivated or at odds with each other in multiple areas. Differences exist between the actual world and the world of the text, no matter how close they may appear. For such reasons, function or intentions of writer and text, critic and text should be examined even if ultimately they are not completely knowable. Going beyond the text, that is, what is "under" or "over" the text, may be as valuable as or more valuable than the text itself.

With reader-response theory in mind, the reader should consider the portraits of the two significant women in *Sum*, Dr. Caroline Ryan and Dr. Elizabeth Elliot. Consciously or unconsciously, the author has portrayed them so as to make comparison inevitable. Clancy draws surface similarities, but the differences between them are so great that the end result is to caricaturize both women. One woman is the epitome of goodness, the other of evil; one, a Mary figure, the other a woman of no purity or valor. Although each is seen separately through most of the novel, events ultimately bring them together in a form of battle. When that occurs, a verbal duel effectively destroys the power of the dark force, Elizabeth Elliot. Virtue and goodness win out, and Cathy Ryan wins the field.

Elizabeth Elliot and Jack Ryan dislike each other intensely. The reason goes back to a confrontation they had before the election of the current president (*Clear*).[3] The narrative style makes it obvious that Ryan reflects the author's attitudes. Neither Ryan nor Clancy seems to find anything praiseworthy in the president's national security adviser, Dr. Elliot. Clancy describes her regular morning mood as "foul" (87), and the remainder of the day seems to bring no improvement. He informs us she doesn't regard it worthwhile to smile at anyone who is nonpolitical. Only those people in a position to advance her point of view get her attention.

As Clancy fills in details about Elizabeth Elliot's character and personality, there appears to be absolutely nobody who likes her. The reader becomes conscious of the author's choice of language to demean Elliot. An Israeli general muses that the American president had "selected superior cabinet officers and personal advisors. Except for Elliot [he] corrected himself" (98). Another time, thinking about the American administration, he labels her the president's "National Security Bitch" (229). A female special agent, "Daga," who is assigned to the president, wants to give the code name Harpy to Dr. Elliot. "Daga didn't like the bitch," writes the author—as if the reader could think otherwise. Elizabeth Elliot is not tough, Daga thinks, even though she is "arrogant" (103). Because of her dislike, Daga doesn't approve of the president's intimate relationship or his infatuation "with the bitch" (188). An assistant to Jack Ryan, Ben Goodley, chooses the same language, describing Elliot as "a prissy, mean-spirited bitch" (564). The Press Corps, looking for a story about the president, hopes he "would do the job for them by marrying the bitch" (579). When Ryan tells the vice president that Elizabeth Elliot is the person who made a serious error about the Russian president, his response is: "Bitch" (754).

With the author's constant use of this derogatory term, the reader cannot help but analyze the author's intentions. Why does he so vilify Dr. Elliot? The language reveals intense dislike, even hatred of her that compels him to draw her as a monster. In doing that he creates a wicked witch character who is utterly without any redeeming qualities. Because of the narrowness of her portrait and the lack of subtlety, she becomes unbelievable to the reader.

The only praise the author allows is for Elliot's appearance, focusing on her good taste in clothing, and her breasts, which are attractive. Clancy appears to have a breast fetish. The subject of breasts comes up often in his books. It is not unusual for Jack or Cathy Ryan to voice interest in breasts. Cathy's breasts are small. Envying women more endowed than herself, "She craved larger ones . . ." (454). Looking at someone at a party, " 'One of hers is worth two of mine,' Cathy noted, managing not to sigh" (534). In a scene in which Ryan at last overcomes his impotency and makes love twice in a single night, the author describes the event: "And then it was over, and he lay at her side. Cathy pulled him against her, his face to her regrettably flat chest" (539). Why "regrettably," and who finds it regrettable? Cathy Ryan? Jack Ryan? Or Clancy?

However, it is only in the breast department that Cathy Ryan is the lesser woman. Evaluating her own appearance, she finds herself reasonably attractive, with blue eyes and fine blond hair, which her husband likes. She has kept her figure. She has a pretty face and attractive legs. But more importantly, she is an understanding wife. When her husband develops a problem with impotency, she treats the problem with delicacy, noting that "the male ego was a fragile thing" (454). Over and over again, she assures herself of Jack Ryan's "goodness," that there is nobody as wonderful as "her" Jack. Of course someone else comes close. That person is Cathy Ryan.

To know her is to love her. She arouses such protective feelings in her colleague, Dr. Bernie Katz, that he'd like to kill her husband for causing her unhappiness. When she asks Dr. Katz pitifully if she lacks something, he wants to shout his declaration of her goodness. Cathy is the best there is. She tells herself she is "a good mother" who plays ball with her son when Jack is away. "She cooked good meals." Further, she does her own housework "or contracted out" (455). Ever the conscientious housewife, in one scene she is shown carrying "a basket of wash" (502). Why is she doing so much housework when she earns so large an income, more than her husband's? They are multimillionaires. Her housewifery makes a strange impression on the reader.

All of these glimpses of Cathy Ryan provide a fascinating contrast with the "bitch" figure Elizabeth Elliot. Cathy Ryan is good tempered while Elliot is not, efficient while Elliot is not, unselfish while Elliot is not. Elliot is firm in her advice to her lover, the president; Cathy is deferential to her husband. She prides herself on not manipulating him (although she takes over calculatedly when she wants another child). Elizabeth Elliot is a completely manipulative woman. Both women enjoy sex, yet Clancy suggests that Cathy Ryan's interest is somehow healthier than Elizabeth Elliot's. For Elliot, sex is mere pleasure, and that is made to seem wrong. For Cathy Ryan, sex is planned and timed so that she can become pregnant again, as she does after Jack Ryan's miraculous recovery from impotency.

The showdown between the two women occurs when they are brought together at a White House party. Both attractive blondes are "dressed almost identically" (533). Why? To the reader it seems Clancy is pointing out the meaninglessness of surface qualities. What he wants to reveal is the inner value of the good woman as opposed to the evil one. By the time they meet, Cathy has regained her sense of self. She zeroes in for the kill, determined to humiliate the woman who almost succeeded in destroying Jack's reputation and career. Face-to-face with Elliot, Cathy Ryan tells the people standing beside them that she and Elliot were at Bennington College at the same time. She brings up stories from those days, making it clear that Elliot was in a radical department and that she slept with a radical, promiscuous professor. Insulting in her put-on pity that Elliot has neither husband nor children, she compares her life to Elliot's. Both are professionals, both entitled to be called "Professor." When Elliot declares her life to be fulfilling, Cathy Ryan delivers her knockout punch. Saying "there's only one real difference between us," she continues: "At home, at night, I sleep with a man." Furthermore, she says, "The nice thing about it is that I never have to change the batteries." Hearing that sly innuendo, Elliot departs "from the battlefield" (536). The good woman has routed the enemy, taken the field, and won a victory for all those who believe in the legitimacy of marriage and motherhood. Clancy's "ideal reader," the one who shares his views of women, might applaud Cathy Ryan's success. The actual reader might question what is "under" the text, the anger behind the writer's characterizations.

NOTES

1. With the television show *Op Center* Clancy was attacked for his portrayal of the Israelis. He protested that he has always been pro-Israel. His writings bear that out, and here is an instance of his views.

2. The 1993 bombing of the World Trade Center in New York by terrorists again showed Clancy to be prophetic. In *The Sum of All Fears*, foreign terrorists are able to enter the United States and bomb a stadium, killing large numbers of people. In *Sum* and *Patriot Games*, Clancy showed that terrorists could penetrate the United States, as they did in the World Trade Center bombing.

3. Roland Green in "A Tom Clancy Concordance, A to Z" (*The Tom Clancy Companion*) writes that Ryan and Elliot "have a loud confrontation which leaves her holding a grudge" (215). Green says nothing about Ryan's animosity toward Elliot after that meeting, a fact which suggests the compiler's biased perspective.

Without Remorse
(1993)

Clancy's agent, Robert Gottlieb, said he thought the 13 to 14 million dollars advance paid by publisher Putnam/Berkley for *Without Remorse* "the biggest amount in the history of publishing for a single book" (Max 1). Yet even Gottlieb's estimate was not complete. Additional foreign sales were expected to make the total advance about 20 million dollars, this at a time of recession in book publication. Publishers have no doubts about the salability of a Clancy novel, even if critics find many faults. Sybil Steinberg's review in *Publishers Weekly*, which could serve as a summary for many others, finds the novel "full of failings of style and moral judgment ... overlong [and] often melodramatic." Nevertheless, it "seems destined to follow its predecessors to the top of the bestseller lists" (59).

Reviewer Gil Schwartz, writing in *Fortune*, calls the novel "dead earnest but deeply wacky." He wonders why Clancy with all his skill in "weaving" together "thousands of incidents and dozens of characters" is not "better" as a writer. Schwartz reiterates evaluations given by critics since the appearance of Clancy's first novel. Always the writer's technology is more interesting than his characters (98). Nevertheless, as with Clancy's other books, Schwartz confesses he found it a page turner. On the other hand, reviewer Daniel Hilbert considers *Without Remorse* less exciting because it is not a typical Clancy novel. "The 'techno' is minimal, and even the 'thriller' is in short supply," he writes. Furthermore, Hilbert doesn't like the major character, John Kelly (known as Clark in other novels). He is too much "a human version of the dazzling, smart technology" at which Clancy is so very good. Where Schwartz forgave the writer his faults because of the excitement of the story, Hilbert does not: "It's a long and violent wait" for the explosion readers "expect from Tom Clancy" (C3).

Can reviewers ever agree about what is pleasurable, memorable, or meaningful in Clancy's fiction? Bob Ellis, also writing in the *Detroit News and Free Press*, counts himself among those disappointed in *The Sum of All Fears*. However, he is also among those won back by this newest Clancy novel. Using a measurement of ten, Ellis writes, *Without Remorse* "rates an eight." Further, he finds the "more than 600 pages . . . practically fat-free" (H7). But Marie Arana-Ward, reviewing the book for the *Washington Post Book World*, takes the opposite view. She lists *Sum* as one of her favorite Clancy books and better than *Without Remorse*, which she finds uneven, with parts of it falling "short of Clancy's norm." Trying to account for what she sees as limitations, she notes that Clancy claims to have started the novel in 1971. Completion, however, didn't come about until twenty years later. Because of the long hiatus, Arana-Ward says, the "earlier chapters" of the novel "ring with a beginner's naivete." Clancy's years of writing experience made all the difference, particularly in the conclusion. "Despite the 500-page boot camp of a preface, the last 100 pages of this novel are the product of a master" (X1).

As always, readers must decide to accept or reject some or all of the reviewers' judgments that concern more than style, length, plot, or characters. Reviewers disagree about the writer's intentions, as well as his philosophy and point of view. Whereas some critics think the book too violent, others do not. Some find too much technology, some too little, and some believe the mix to be just right. Whatever position an individual reader takes, there is probably a critical view to support it. Nevertheless, it seems clear that *Without Remorse* stands apart from other Clancy novels in many ways.

PLOT DEVELOPMENT

Two plots exist side by side in the novel, both introduced at the beginning. Further, each is intended to reflect and symbolize the other, though at first that would seem impossible because of the subject matter. One traces the war of an individual against drug dealers. The second is about a phase of the war in Vietnam. It tells of U.S. efforts to rescue a group of American military POWs held in a Vietnamese prison. Someone unfamiliar with the novel or the author's characteristic techniques might wonder how such disparate plots could be linked together at all, much less in a meaningful way. However, Clancy succeeds in doing that and in a manner atypical of his other work.

In each novel, the author brings together the various parts, no matter how many or how unrelated they may appear to the reader. Ultimately, they mesh, usually satisfactorily, after a suspenseful and action-packed conclusion. *Without Remorse* is no exception to that. One major difference in this novel, though, is the smaller number of plots. Another important change comes in the early connection between the plots. As a result of these two notable alterations of pattern, the reader is able to follow the twists and turns of the story lines readily. Because of the tighter bridging, the book is a much faster read than Clancy's other books.

The Two Plots

John Kelly, the major figure, serves as the link between the plot about drugs and the plot about rescuing prisoners of war. Moving back to an earlier time period than previous Clancy novels or the one that follows *(Debt of Honor)*, the story is set in the early 1970s. The United States is still embroiled in a hot war in Vietnam and a cold war with the Soviet Union. At home the drug culture has exploded.[1]

The Drug Plot

When the story opens, John Kelly, a highly decorated ex-navy man, is enjoying civilian life as a married man and soon-to-be-father. His happiness comes to an abrupt end following the death of his pregnant wife in a car accident. Six months after that he picks up a young hitchhiker named Pam and takes her back with him to the island and boat on which he lives. Kelly soon learns that Pam has escaped from a group of drug dealers who abused her and forced her into prostitution. Sick and fearful for her life, she piques Kelly's compassion and interest, and, within a very short time, his love. Once again he has someone to live for. But, as reviewer Bob Ellis writes, Kelly "keeps losing the women he loves" (H7).

A combination of naiveté about drug dealers, carelessness, and pride leads Kelly to take chances that bring about Pam's death. He comes close to dying as well but is saved by the brilliant surgical skills of a friend, Sam Rosen, and the dedicated care of nurse Sandy O'Toole. When newspaper accounts and detectives reveal information about the brutal murder of Pam, Kelly vows to strike back. He becomes the avenger, tracking and exterminating all the people who played a role in her degradation and death. Using his varied skills and marine training, Kelly destroys a Baltimore drug ring, its dealers and top man, as well as the corrupt police detective who has helped keep them in business.

The Vietnam Plot

Before resigning from military service, Kelly, then a navy SEAL, participated in a rescue mission in Vietnam. He brought out a navy pilot after encountering and surviving the most grueling circumstances possible. Awarded a medal and promoted to chief, Kelly was encouraged to train to become an officer, but he declined. However, his military service is not really over. He has one more covert job to do in Vietnam, where a group of twenty American military men are being held prisoner. Although the men have been reported as dead, reconnaissance photos show otherwise. Brave, risk-taking officers decide it is their moral duty to liberate the men. Using subterfuge, deception, whatever it takes to achieve a just mission, they persuade the president to agree to a secret action.

Because of his background and knowledge of the terrain, even though he is no longer with the military, Kelly is brought into planning the rescue mission. This takes place while he is eliminating the drug dealers one or two at a time until only the top people are left. When told he is the only person who knows the area in Vietnam where the prisoners are held, Kelly volunteers to go back. With a group of specially trained marines, who have also volunteered for the action, he returns to Vietnam. Unbeknownst to them, the mission has been treacherously exposed to the Russians by two Americans opposed to the war. When the Russians alert the Vietnamese, the rescue effort fails. Kelly manages to escape, and fortunately he captures a Russian colonel, whom he takes back to America. The colonel has been using unusual and devious methods to obtain information about American military matters from a POW in the camp. The capture of the colonel proves to be brilliant strategy.

Through Machiavellian maneuvers on the part of the planners of the rescue action, the mission ultimately is saved. Politics and diplomacy are utilized. The Russian is sent home in exchange for the freedom of the American prisoners. By the time the purpose of Kelly's activities is fulfilled successfully, he has also finished the job he gave himself, to avenge the death of Pam. He has hunted down and killed the last of the drug dealers, as well as the corrupt policeman who protected them. And although many people know about his activities, Kelly is safe. Recruited by the CIA, given a fake set of fingerprints for his old Kelly file, and renamed John Clark, he begins a new life.

As the book ends, Kelly, now Clark, views on television the arrival at Clark Air Force Base of the freed American prisoner, Colonel Robin Zacharias, whom he saved. Because of Kelly, "all twenty" (639) of the American prisoners are coming back. Watching with him is his wife, the former Sandy O'Toole, pregnant with their first child. The story has come full circle.

CHARACTERS

Although Kelly is the only major character in the novel, there are numerous people in the two plots. Some, though named, make only a brief appearance, whereas others have roles important to the unfolding of the stories. They do not cross lines from one plot to the other. Only Kelly does that. Various men are familiar figures from earlier Clancy novels, where they were shown at the height or end of their careers. Here many of them are still advancing in the career pattern and do not have the power or prestige of later years.

Military and Government Figures

Admiral James Greer is known to Clancy readers. In four books he mentored Jack Ryan at the CIA. Although Greer died in the course of *Clear and Present Danger*, in *Without Remorse* he has just started working at the CIA. Greer has lost his son in the Vietnam War, as has his friend, Admiral Casmir Podulski, who appears only in this novel. Podulski is part of the group that plans the rescue mission, but he dies of a heart attack before the full completion of the activity. His wife, having lost both husband and only child, commits suicide. (It is plausible to see her as yet another victim of the Vietnam War.) Admiral Maxwell, the third navy man in the group, takes the greatest risk to his position. With his future dependent on success, it is suggested that the seeming failure of the mission destroys any possibility of salvaging his job. Like Podulski, he has a role only in this book. Another person known to Clancy fans is Robert Ritter, who works for the CIA. Daring, willing to take chances, even to lie when necessary to save American lives, Ritter seems much more honorable here than in *Clear and Present Danger*. In that novel some of his behavior appeared questionable, at best, and his worry about American lives then less important than political concerns. The change in Ritter over time makes one wonder if the novelist sees him as growing cynical with age.

Druggies, Detectives, and Doctors

Drug dealers are part of the Baltimore landscape Clancy describes. Much alike in attitude and appearance, they are not memorable unless shown in some particularly grisly scene. They prey on young, vulnerable women, turning them into prostitutes and addicts. Any woman who disobeys is gang-raped and sometimes murdered. Rape comes easily to these men, as does murder. When ordered by their boss to kill one of their own people, they do it without compunction. Betrayal means nothing. Most of them are animalistic, unthinking brutes, stalking the jungle the city has become. Only the schemers, the planners who employ the pushers, survive for any length of time, but Kelly outsmarts them all, and, without remorse, kills everyone involved in the ring that brutalized Pam.

Most of the detectives are hardworking, honest, reliable men. Faced with overwhelming numbers of hoodlums, they do their best to solve crimes, but success often eludes them. Some members of the force are naive or unsuspecting, and because of that, innocent people are victimized by corrupt policemen. One such person in the novel is Detective Mark Charon, an officer in the pay of drug dealers. Charon resembles some real policemen whose depraved activities have become familiar in the drug scene. Like them, for a long period of time Charon has managed to protect certain dealers and himself from exposure and to grow rich in the process. Ultimately, however, he is shot by the dealer he has shielded. This is ironic, but there is a further irony. Even in death Charon is protected by his police peers, and the facts of his dishonesty are not revealed to the press or public.

In what has become a practice, Clancy includes a physician who is a kind, friendly, clever, sentimental man, outstanding in his field. He is usually Jewish, thus giving the author the opportunity to display his knowledge of a Yiddish word or two.[2] In *Remorse* the doctor is Sam Rosen, and he saves Kelly's life when he is shot by drug pushers. Rosen frets and fusses over Kelly, trying to protect and defend him. A stereotypical figure, Sam Rosen is married to a pharmacologist even more stereotypical than he. She is "short, overweight" and speaks "in a New York accent" (43). So enamored (or forgetful) is Clancy of his description that he repeats it a few pages later: "She was rather a dumpy woman, short and overweight." Worse, "she looked like the kind of woman who, behind the wheel of a car, attracts the hatred of male drivers" (59). It is unclear what the author intends by that statement. But with all that against her, Clancy draws Sarah Rosen as the usual version of a Jewish mother figure, a caring worrier.

Traitors

Two young New Englanders, Wally Hicks and Peter Henderson, get in over their heads in a treasonous game. They had been friends at Andover Academy, one going on to Harvard, the other to Brown. After graduation, both came to Washington, Hicks on the White House staff, Henderson as a senatorial aide. "Theirs was a fat and lazy time for American youth." Both "wealthy families had insulated" the two "from reality with the privilege that money could buy without imparting the wisdom required for its proper use" (228). The author suggests that wealth and privilege have destroyed their true sense of humanity, that they value their ideas and theories over people. Their dialogue reveals them as snobs and "peaceniks," who are contemptuous about the military. Hicks and Henderson do not see the "little people," that is, average Americans, as smart enough to understand diplomacy over guns. Putting themselves above those little people, as well as the government, the two betray their trust. Hicks dies, but Henderson survives. Other novels set in a later period show him to have been coerced into playing a double agent.

Kelly/Clark

Never before have we seen so much of John Kelly, and it is not likely we will again, even though Clancy returns him to his role as CIA agent in the next book. Large, handsome, powerful, clever, resourceful, one almost runs out of adjectives to describe Kelly. He seems to be superb at everything he undertakes, especially physical tasks. An expert in diving, swimming, running, weaponry, map reading, languages, navigation, and disguises, there is little he cannot do. About the same age as the treasonous Hicks and Henderson, Kelly is imbued with what the omniscient author obviously sees as "the right stuff," that is, the "right" values. The son of a fireman who dies in the line of duty, Kelly did not come from wealth and prestige as did Hicks and Henderson. Where they attended one of the most prestigious but secular prep schools, Kelly is the product of Jesuit education. With the Jesuits he honed his intelligence—and his grammar, as one admiral notes. His IQ is genius level at 147. Yet Kelly did not go to college. Instead, like his father before him, he joined the navy.

Kelly is a strong leader, with the philosophy that things happen in war and "somebody has to get it [the job] done" (203). Taking the same attitude about his activities at home, he asks, "And when the law doesn't work, then what?" (409). Kelly's reasoning and language recall the Irangate hearings of the Reagan administration. His statements might be called the Fawn Hall position. Hall lectured Congress on the need for people to take things into their own hands if the law didn't work.[3]

Kelly puts people before the law and doesn't try to protect himself at the expense of others. Willing to put his life on the line, he believes good men have to stand up for patriotism, justice, and their fellow Americans. Yet, for all his fine qualities, there is what some critics have labelled the "amoral" side. He behaves as a vigilante when he seeks retaliation for Pam's death, not trusting the police to do the job. He breaks the law again and again for what he considers justice but others consider murder. "It's only murder when innocent people die," says Kelly (628).

Kelly's "dark side" is symbolized by the frequent reference to transformation of his face and eyes, changes he tries to hide. These features become "old and feral and ugly" (133) when he learns of criminal actions. At such times he is frightening, even bestial. Seeing him is "like opening the door of a cage" (360). The eyes may be ice cold or may burn with rage, but hot or cold, they are frightening to most watchers. Those who ignore such warning signs do so at their peril.

One of the murderous drug dealers finds it amusing when Kelly, revealing a tender side, weeps over his graphic descriptions of Pam's death. He had wept before, in love and gratitude to Pam, who for a brief time offered him hope of finding a new life with a new love. When he weeps in front of the drug dealer, it is his reaction to the pain of loss. The act is misinterpreted. The dealer, thinking him weak and unmasculine, mocks Kelly. He cannot envision the horrific and violent death Kelly has planned for him, a slow death as his body disintegrates bit by bit in a decompression chamber.

In the final scene of the novel, the Epilogue, Kelly weeps once more, as he watches on television the return of the prisoners he helped save. The author describes him as "seeing the joy that really could replace pain, no matter how vast" (639). This Epilogue follows the last nerve-racking actions of the story, in which a related point has been made. A deadly boat race is underway between Kelly, the Coast Guard, and the police. If Kelly eludes them and gets to the navy sailboat waiting for him, he will be free, reborn as Clark. Kelly, in a feat of derring-do, outwits and deceives his pursuers. One Coast Guardsman says: "There's always a winner and always a loser" (633).[4] Ironically, the watchers think Kelly has gone to a watery grave and that they are victorious. But things are not so clearly black and white, even though the reader knows the quarry has foiled them. Clancy does not do Kelly justice in the Epilogue when he suggests that joy replaces pain. Kelly may find happiness again, but the pain of loss will always be part of him. Clancy's other novels remind us of that. Kelly's life, unlike that of Clancy's sunnier hero Jack Ryan of other novels, is a composite of suffering and joy. In the end, the reader sees Kelly as both winner and loser.

STYLE

Playing with Names

At several points in the novel, Clancy introduces the name of James Bond as a source of humor. Bond jokes are made about Kelly, and details about Bond are mentioned from time to time. On occasion, though, to understand the reference the reader must either have read author Ian Fleming's novels or seen the Bond movies. Clancy plays other name games as well, sometimes to tweak the reader. There is a detective named Ryan, not Jack Ryan, but Emmet Ryan, Jack's father, but we hear nothing about Jack.

Using Latin, the author humorously shows a Russian spy who mocks gays, speculating that the code name Cassius is a misnomer for Henderson. According to the spy, he should be called Casca, the female version of the name. To catch the joke, the reader must know declensions. The reader who is aware of the foreign aspect of the name game might also recognize from Greek mythology the name "Charon." Clancy bestows that name on his corrupt detective. Charon was the son of Erebus (primeval darkness) and Styx (nymph of the river that flows into the lower world). Charon is the dark sailor who ferries souls of the dead across the River Styx to the underworld. In *Remorse* the name Charon aptly fits the detective whose secret life supports the purveyors of drugs and death.

Two other names the author tosses in as a teaser are Archie and Jughead. Cartoon readers and computer users of the Internet system immediately recognize the names, but for others the joke goes unnoticed. Not all names are meant for fun, though, but names are significant to the writer in various ways. The name Doris seems to irritate Kelly (and Clancy?). Driving the Washington Beltway, Kelly reflects about a girl named Doris, and this thought comes to mind: "What a dumb name" (414). Why? The reader is given no clue. Another unhappy name in the Clancy lexicon is Marvin. Clancy seems to save that one for terrorists or spies. Marvin is the pseudonym for the KGB Russian spy to whom Henderson reports in Washington. It is also the name of the American Indian terrorist in *The Sum of All Fears*.

THEME: THE PARALLEL WARS

Without Remorse, unlike Clancy's other novels, does not have multiple divergent themes. This book, which might be considered Clancy's Vietnam novel, is entirely about war, war at home and war abroad. No matter what kind of war we engage in, the theme is that all wars resemble each other. Even as the author examines some of the issues of Vietnam, he enlarges the scope to include another kind of war. He intends the two plots to parallel each other because they are both parts of the same theme.

War produces honorable people and traitors; victims and victimizers; goodness and brutality; morality, immorality, and amorality. The theme underscores the necessity of taking a stand against evil wherever it is found. Even if evil can't be eradicated completely, Americans must stand guard on all fronts.

The drug war and the Vietnam War produce victims of all kinds as they kill, maim, and destroy everything in their path. However, it is the young, the children, the innocent girls in both wars who provoke the strongest feelings in Kelly. When he see a young girl in Baltimore hooked on drugs and forced into prostitution, her behavior reminds him of scenes in Vietnam. This is what war brings to a civilian population. Kelly remembers "the way the villagers moved. . . . Resigned, automatic motion, like living robots. . . . They would have moved the same way to their deaths" (271). The violence of the drug pushers toward the girls who are their "mules" resembles that of the enemy Vietnamese toward their own people. Gang rape is common on both fronts, in Baltimore and Vietnam. Weapons and brutality settle all accounts. Kindness, decency, and honor are nonexistent.

Though different in most ways, the Russian and Vietnamese military and the drug rings in Baltimore have their chains of command. Both are shown in action. Spies form part of each operation. The Russians and Vietnamese spy on each other, and everyone spies on the Americans. In the drug war, pushers and dealers distrust everyone. Like people in other organizations, they want to get to the top and, like the Russians and Communist Vietnamese, will use any method to do so. The enemy on both fronts lacks morality.

Periodically, the author reminds us of the connection between the two plots and therefore the two wars. Wherever possible, he uses one to call the reader's attention to the other. He wants the reader to recognize that drug users are also traitors. An instance is seen with the treacherous White House staff aide, Wally Hicks, a frequent drug user. When Hicks's treason is discovered, Kelly is given the task of dealing with it. He knows Hicks must die. Poetic justice is served when Kelly gives Hicks the option of being killed or taking a drug overdose for an easy death.

People Kelly meets also have their own connection to the Vietnam War, but always there is a linkage to both wars. The nurse, Sandy O'Toole, who takes care of Kelly in the hospital after he is shot by the drug pushers, is the widow of a man killed in the war. (When both plots are resolved, Sandy and Kelly marry.) Another pairing of the plots comes through a young drug-taking prostitute named Doris, whose brother also died in the war. Doris's father collapsed emotionally because of his son's death. His anguish led to alienation from his remaining child, Doris, who ran away from home only to become a victim of the drug dealers. Again and again, the author makes the point that drugs mean death. Ironically, the drug known as "Asian Sweet" is brought to the United States inside the bodies of servicemen killed in Vietnam.

Kelly worries about his involvement in the two wars at the same time.

Yet he knows he cannot give up either action until there is a successful conclusion. Highlighting the final parallel between the two stories, the author brings both of Kelly's roles to an end at about the same time. Nevertheless he raises questions about closure. Can there ever be an end to the bitterness brought about by the Vietnam War? Clancy doesn't answer that. And that other war, the war with drugs, is never settled. Good people can only try, but like the military they must always be vigilant.

ALTERNATE READING: MYTH CRITICISM

Throughout time writers have used myths as a means of explaining history and human behavior. Myths provide models and structure for literature. However, no single methodology of myth theory exists. Each writer chooses from past stories—characters and episodes—what seems most meaningful for a present work.

Myth criticism is "not so much a critical approach in literary studies as the convergence of several methods and forms of inquiry" concerning the relationship of "literature and myth" (Reeves 520). Some critics regard myth as a symbolic way of thinking about the world, of understanding it imagistically. Others see it as a representation of history. Both views are part of myth criticism.

Much of myth criticism comes from the theories of Swiss psychologist Carl Jung. Although Jung's studies have been called "archetypal criticism" (archetypes are patterns of images which are part of the collective unconscious), they are so much a part of myth theory that the terms are used interchangeably. Archetypal and myth criticism are concerned with the universality of experience that touches individuals. Myth critics find patterns that have existed over extensive periods in many forms and cultures. Every century has seen the use of myths, for they provide recognizable symbols of people and objects. Among the figures are the scapegoat, the sinner, the hero, the earth mother, the fallen woman/whore. Familiar nonhuman elements are unusual kinds of rivers, wastelands, the underworld. Rituals and even numerology are associated with myth. Mythical characters stand outside the ordinary human mode in their power for good or ill. Through them readers comprehend the world that in its complexity would elude their understanding without myth.

Clancy does not alert the reader to his use of myth. Rather, toward the end of the book, he suggests the novel be seen as tragedy. "He (Kelly) remembered high school English classes. . . . Aristotle's rules of tragedy. The hero had to have a tragic flaw. . . . Kelly's flaw . . . he loved too much, cared too much, invested too much in the things and the people who touched his life. He could not turn away" (593–594). Perhaps Kelly is a type of tragic hero, but not in the Aristotelian sense. Because his flaw does not destroy him, the people around him, or the world he inhabits, the rules of tragedy do not apply. As seen in the outcome of the novel, Kelly may be a loser, but he is also a winner. That in itself would prevent his being a tragic hero. In fact, Kelly fits more into the mythic model than the tragic one. He is a larger-than-life hero who, like the mythical phoenix, "dies" only to be "reborn."

Kelly is a hero of the James Bond variety, and critics have noted Bond's mythic characteristics. Has Clancy recognized the similarities and pointed up the resemblances by his frequent humorous references to Bond? Perhaps it is the opposite, that by joking he has tried to deflect the reader's seeing both Kelly and Bond as brothers under the skin, both indestructible heroes. Reviewers have described Kelly as the "dark side" of Ryan (and of Clancy), and a link may be found between them.

In the discussion of *Patriot Games* (see chapter 5) the characteristics of a fairy tale are described. On the surface *Without Remorse*, a ferocious and savage story, would seem an unlikely candidate for a similar label. Yet, an examination of the markers reveals a sameness, albeit with a modernist script. Violence, though disguised or sugarcoated, is part of the fairy tale and mythical world in which cruelty, bestiality, and betrayal are accepted. In *Remorse* the same elements exist, and the mythological requirements are fulfilled, though updated.

Unlike *Patriot Games* and the Bond novels, *Without Remorse* is complicated by its two unrelated sets of enemies, the North Vietnamese abroad and the drug dealers at home. However, the double plot does not alter the ability of the hero to overcome all odds on both fronts. Both groups threaten the "kingdom," that is, the United States, though in different ways. The communists in Asia, abetted by Russian communists, are fighting a physical and psychological war against POWs. As in the Bond novels, the enemy is non-Anglo-Saxon (Russian, Asian) and has a "foreign" and therefore unattractive appearance (Clancy's description of the Vietnamese) or unappealing traits (the Russians). Most important, though, is their evil nature, from which the free world must be saved. The foreign enemies are automatons, programed to commit inhumane acts with no thought of mercy. The other enemy, the drug dealers, is also totally wicked. Except for varying levels of intelligence, all of the dealers and pushers are cut from one cloth. They, like the enemy abroad, are the "black hats" who must be eliminated. Their cupidity, their villainy knows no limits. Even in their brutality they are perverted.

The hero, Kelly, is a "white hat." As mythical hero, only he can change things. Cast in the role of St. George, dragon-slayer and patron saint of England, he is like Bond or Ryan, but unlike them he has a hydra-headed dragon to slay. For the different tasks he must be two men. In his military persona, because only he has both the knowledge and ability to rescue American prisoners, he must enter the dragon's cage alone. For that battle he is officially employed, like Bond and Ryan in their many jobs. As a military hero who understands duty and sacrifice Kelly is willing to risk his life. American military groups back him up as numerous British groups do Bond. But ultimately, in each case, the battle is won or lost by the lone hero. Still, the victory of each hero is temporary. For Bond and Kelly the enemy returns at some future time, when the hero must take up the sword again. Kelly's "sword" is the best that modern technology can provide. That technology, embodied in such daring inventions as the "sled" Kelly uses to get into Vietnam waters, reminds moviegoers of the spectacular gadgetry of the Bond movies.

In his other persona as avenging knight, Kelly is totally alone. He has no support system to help him eliminate the dealers, and the killings place him in conflict with people who would be his friends and allies under different circumstances. Discouraged at times by the seemingly endless and lonely struggle, he perseveres. He proves himself a one-man army who cuts off the limbs—the pushers and assistants—and then lopes off the head of the dragon—the top man. Unlike Bond, Kelly has no one to fashion weapons of any sort for him. He must design or alter everything he needs to overcome all odds. His ingenuity is amazing in weaponry and disguises. For example, in this role, we see him turn diving equipment into an instrument of death, and once again it calls up memories of Bond's daring devices.

Kelly is seen as the single hero, the only one who can win the battle over evil. With his dark, romantic good looks and inscrutable demeanor Kelly fits into the pattern of the archetypal knight/prince/wanderer from whom the Bond character was drawn before him. Such a figure has developed from myth and literature over centuries. Sometimes, however, the term "Byronic hero" is used to describe that kind of man. He is the melancholy loner whose life has been destroyed by terrible events. He is a sinner who carries an enormous burden of guilt. From this design Kelly is modeled. But mention has been made of another myth, the rise of the phoenix from ashes to begin anew. This myth too is applicable to Kelly. Following the death of his wife Kelly attempts to rebuild, only to have his happiness destroyed a second time. It is not until his third try that resolution comes at last.[5]

Like a quest hero of fairy tales, Kelly is tested over and over. He must overcome one trial after another until final victory is his. In the military field, that does not come until the prisoners are returned home. In the drug war, each battle brings him closer to the end, until finally he shoots the leader of the ring, which is like the symbolic cutting off of the head of the dragon. With both tasks completed, he has earned his reward. And rewarded he is, in the tradition of the fairy tale. Kelly wins the heart and then the hand of the reluctant Sandy O'Toole, who learns to see him as he truly is, gallant, noble, daring. As the sorrow of the past subsides, he will find the happiness that has eluded him. Another gift is on its way, the birth of a child. At the end, the promise of a new life symbolizes hope. Birth is related to the rise of the phoenix. Once again Clancy winds up this novel with the prospect of a child, much as he did *Patriot Games*.[6]

NOTES

1. Although drugs were not new to the United States, much of the present proliferation began during the Vietnam War. People who had never before been exposed to drugs found them readily and cheaply in Asia. They became the customers also for Columbian drugs. In America, drug taking became one of the elements of the social and cultural "revolution" of the 1960s and 1970s, at first a sign of the protest and rebellion of young people.

2. Unfortunately, the effect of this is wooden and out of character. The author does not limit himself to Jewish words. In his next novel, he does the same thing with Japanese.

3. Fawn Hall was secretary to Oliver North, who served the White House as an aide, first to National Security Advisor Robert McFarlane and then to his successor, Admiral John Poindexter.

4. The Coast Guardsman is Chief Quartermaster Manuel Oreza, nicknamed Portagee. He is seen in *Clear and Present Danger* and also in *Debt of Honor*.

5. The number three itself is often associated with magic, myth, or religion.

6. In *Patriot Games*, however, the baby is born before the story ends.

Debt of Honor
(1994)

When editor/novelist/reviewer Christopher Buckley critiqued Clancy's eighth novel, a short war of words erupted between the two writers. To Buckley this altercation was funny. To Clancy it was not, although after the skirmish became public, he asserted the "faxes [which he sent Buckley] were meant as a joke" (Mansfield, 6 Oct. 1994:B1+). Buckley had made a number of provocative statements about both the book and Clancy's writing, but undoubtedly he sank his most piercing barb when he called Clancy "the James Fenimore Cooper of his day, which is to say, the most successful bad writer of his generation. This is no mean feat, for there are many, many more rich bad writers today than there were in Cooper's time" (2 Oct. 1994, sec. 7:28).

Not as stinging as Buckley, other reviewers of the novel list some of the familiar pluses and minuses. "The mastery of minutia can become tedious in a 768-page novel" writes Steve Jones in *USA Today*. Yet, he continues, the ending of the book is "stunning" (D1). Reviewer Kristiana Helmick also praises the "page-turning climax," finding it "gripping," but "given such a ponderous volume to slog through, one barely gets there" (15). Generally, Jones's and Helmick's comments are representative of those who find the book entertaining but overly long and too didactic. Although reviewers bemoan the numerous plots and settings, they praise the novelist's deftness in bringing everything together. Some point to the author's prescience, others to his understanding of global

economic issues, and others, as always, to his mastery of military technology. Judy Shelton, a research fellow at the Hoover Institute, also
praises the economic utility of the work. She calls the novel "a boomer,"
assuring the reader of the entertainment value of a work dealing with
"currency turmoil, bond market volatility, trade wars, financial panic
and economic collapse" (H1).

Not only is the style familiar to Clancy readers, but so too are many
of the characters and parts of the plot. The enemy may have changed,
no longer Russia but Japan, yet the driving forces of money, land, and
power are much the same. Where Russia's (the former Soviet Union)
expansionism was labeled "Communism," it differed little from the old
type of colonialism and imperialism of Europe and Asia. However, with
the dissolution of the Soviet Union, the power and influence of its individual regions have been diminished. In *Debt of Honor* Clancy describes
the same attitudes that once promoted the increase of Soviet power and
influence, but now they spur the military and economic attacks of Japan.

With the cold war over, the Soviet Union dissolved, and Russia weak-
ened in actual fact, the novelist focuses on Japan, portraying it as the
most threatening country for the United States. The economic issues and
trade relationships between Japan and the United States are real current
events.[1] But Clancy fictionalizes the military preparedness of Japan, making it resemble the aggressive former Soviet states. Once again air and
sea battles take place, not in European or Russian territory this time, but
in the Pacific basin. Submarines, surface warships, air carriers go to war.
Nuclear missiles, no longer a threat from the Russians, are part of the
secret Japanese arsenal. An unprovoked attack by Japan occurs, and war
is under way without being declared. In much that happens there is a
certain familiarity, a reminder of the Japanese attack on Pearl Harbor,
Hawaii, in December 1941. New military alliances are formed between
the United States and Russia to prevent decimation by the Japanese. The
hostilities and takeovers are military and economic in the novel, but both
menace world peace. All these events may create a certain sense of déjà
vu for a Clancy reader. Have we seen some of this before? Are we reading another *Red Storm Rising*, which has become *Rising Sun Arises?*

PLOT DEVELOPMENT

The heart of the story concerns trade relationships between Japan and
the United States. Each country suspects the other's economic policies,

although on the surface the two nations are allies. Business interests are at odds over protectionist laws and the competition for markets. The situation is comparable to a dry forest ready for a match to ignite a fire. That eruption comes through an unexpected event, when two fatal automobile accidents occur in the United States. Two Japanese cars containing flawed gas tanks explode on impact, killing several Americans. The tragedy provides the opportunity for American manufacturers to seek harsh trading restrictions against Japan, which has had the upper hand in many commercial dealings. When feelings get whipped up in the United States, punitive economic laws are enacted.

The Japanese immediately feel the pinch as their exports are threatened, and their economy slides downhill. They will not allow the United States to control their lives. Remembering the devastation of World War II and their struggles afterward, they suffer from a type of paranoia. Although they rebuilt and gained a strong position among nations, some factions believe they still are too much under the control of foreigners. Furthermore, some imperialistic groups in Japan have never given up the idea of more land and more power. These groups, composed primarily of the business community, have with careful planning taken over the government, silenced the opposition, and built an arsenal of nuclear weapons. Once the U.S. Congress passes hostile trade limitations, the militant forces in Japan decide the time is ripe for action. They launch an economic attack that almost destroys the world economy while at the same time they strike out militarily. Japan invades the American flag possessions, the Mariana Islands, destroys American submarines, and threatens its neighbors and the United States with nuclear warfare. The U.S. government decides she must be stopped.

To avoid total war with Japan the United States has to move quickly and cleverly, even though both America and its new ally, Russia, have depleted their military strengths. Russia has sold its nuclear missiles to Japan and its military forces are in disarray. The United States has much of its fleet in mothballs and not enough people to run ships or fly planes. Nevertheless, the American government (mostly Jack Ryan) and military leaders with savvy, subterfuge, and quick-wittedness win out. The economy is restored, nuclear weapons are destroyed, and the American islands of the Pacific are regained. Peace is recovered, but at a great price. The seething anger that has been held inside some Japanese demands atonement. A return to the old situation will not do. A lone Japanese pilot bombs the U.S. Capitol, showing how vulnerable an open and free country can be. The mind-boggling result of that single suicide attack is destruction of the government, making Jack Ryan president. Clancy has prepared the ground for his next novel, in which presumably we'll see Ryan in office.

Subplots

The minor plots in *Debt* serve little purpose except to highlight the problems and stressful nature of the presidency. Although two of the several subplots in the novel are more fully developed and more memorable than the others, even they have a limited relationship to the major plot. Both involve sex and sexual misconduct in the U.S. and Japanese governments. In Washington, a former senator, now the vice-president, is accused of drugging and raping a former aide of his. Almost nothing comes of this plot, but it works as a deus ex machina—god of the machine, a familiar device used to manipulate endings in classical plays. Toward the end of the novel the resignation of the vice president allows Jack Ryan to accept his job, a role he never fills since he immediately becomes president when the government is destroyed. In Japan, another subplot concerns the electability of Hiroshi Goto as prime minister. Goto's mistress is a young American runaway. Because the businessmen who control Goto want no scandal associated with him, the mistress is dispatched brutally.

CHARACTERS

Although many of the American characters are known to the reader, most of the Japanese characters are newly constructed. The majority of the Americans fall under the Clancy rubric "good guys," wherever they reside, whereas most of the Japanese are "bad guys." The major American characters appear more frequently, in more detail, and in more episodes than the Japanese. Though not very complex, the Americans are more so than the Japanese, who are invariably one-dimensional and flat, formulaic, even cartoonlike figures. The two significant Japanese figures, Prime Minister Hiroshi Goto and controlling businessman Raizo Yamata, are stereotypical renditions of the enemy abroad—evil, cruel, vindictive men.

Government Leaders: American

Roger Durling, seen previously as vice president in *The Sum of All Fears* now is president of the United States. An able and thoughtful man, he wisely employs Jack Ryan as his national security adviser. It is good that he takes that action because Durling is a cautious person who needs someone like Ryan, more daring and outspoken, as well as more knowledgeable about almost everything than anyone. Durling makes a clever and skillful president, yet even he is not in Ryan's league. Durling has decided to run for a second term with his vice-president, Edward Kealty, again. Then information comes about Kealty which changes his plans.

Kealty has been an asset to Durling's administration up to the time charges of sexual harassment are brought to the president's attention. Suddenly, his past activities threaten to bring down the administration. A man of considerable sexual appetite, Kealty has been involved with a number of women. Until one woman decides to go public, Kealty has been able to keep his activities secret. Now the accusations against him could reverberate against the current White House occupant. Not only is he accused of drugging and raping a woman, but also of seducing several. One woman was so disturbed by the experience she committed suicide. Although actions of sexual assault often lead to court cases, Kealty escapes prosecution, at least in this book. The administration wants to avoid embarrassment in an election year. Newspapers leak the story, but Kealty is permitted to resign his post.

Kealty is one of several politicians in the novel who strike a chord of recognition in the reader. Although the name is a fiction, most of his alleged activities are not Clancy's invention. For several years the Senate Ethics Committee investigated sexual harassment charges brought against a prominent Western senator. The story of his drugging and raping a young woman he knew got prominent attention from the newspapers. After that revelation, a number of women (including some who had worked for him) came forward with accusations against the senator. Kealty is punished by removal from office, a fate similar to that of the real senator, who was pressured to resign. The character's activities alert the reader to the hints associated with Kealty's name, and the initials, EK, to the author's choice of another senator. Caution stands behind the change of initials for the fictionalized—though obvious—senator from the West. However, the author's use of another actual senator's first name and last initial, as well as the New England area Kealty is said to come from, surely is deliberate. That other senator's name also has been associated with unsavory sexual reports. The author seems to be striking two birds with a single stone, hitting both Democrats and Republicans in the naming and story of Kealty. As readers have seen in the novel *Without Remorse*, Clancy's naming often has meaning.

The totally upright hero of the novel, Jack Ryan, is playing golf with his old friend Robby Jackson at the Greenbrier Hotel (a typical authorial use of local color) when he is summoned to the White House. He immediately leaves the famous resort hotel in the mountains of West Virginia to return to Washington. It seems that Ryan, once again, is absolutely essential to the functioning of his government, and he immediately responds to the call of duty. He has been out of government for two years, leading the life of a rich businessman. Being a broker turns out to be an unexpected bonus when a group of Japanese businessmen start the economic war that almost destroys the banks of the world. Ryan knows all the ins and outs of Wall Street. Because of his background he immediately understands information given him about computer manipulation of the market and the consequences. His logical mind links the economic to the military actions, so that he comes up quickly with a plan to solve the economic problems. Not long after that, Ryan decodes the mystery behind the martial strategies of Japan. Once he clarifies those two parts of the puzzle, it is time to take action on all fronts. As in previous novels, Ryan goes on the offensive, lecturing those who would do nothing or go slowly. He instructs the presidential staff (and sometimes even the president) about history and the founding principles of the country, stressing the debt of honor owed those who support it. Always more convincing, more passionate, and more honorable than others among the president's men, he persuades the president to act more quickly than is Durling's inclination.

Should readers not appreciate Ryan sufficiently, there are frequent reminders of his many abilities. Without Ryan's brilliance and daring in protecting the country against the actions of a former president out of control (*Sum*), Durling would not now be president (21). He doesn't seem at all resentful of Ryan's frequent sermons. Indeed he constantly praises his national security adviser: "You're a good man in a storm" (243). Durling (or the author) finds the statement so expressive that he repeats it at other times (540, 684). In the midst of crisis after crisis, President Durling takes time out to think of Ryan's talents. No matter that Ryan has a temper, Durling muses. His adviser can be completely cool and controlled when necessary, a man with "good brains, good instinct, and a cool head when needed" (684). The president also likes Ryan's ability to tell a joke even though he takes his work very seriously. The reader should note that Durling's impressions of Ryan, the physical posture when he is tense, his voice, his joking, and his directness are characteristics of the author himself.[2]

Durling is not alone in thinking Ryan exceptional. The presidential special secret service agent informs Ryan that she likes him because "I don't have to explain security to you like I do with everybody else" (373). That is because he thinks the way she does, like an agent. Ryan's own bodyguard finds "no pomposity" in him (475). A Wall Street whiz believes "That Ryan guy is pretty smart" (492). Senators of both parties take time to laud him. He's a "bright boy" (740) who has done much for the president, according to both Democrats and Republicans. Ryan is not only smarter than the secretary of state, but also more rational. After an irritating exchange with the secretary, Ryan reminds himself that the man comes from Yale, where a logic course is "probably an elective." He, on the other hand, is a graduate of Boston College, a Jesuit school, where such a course "had been mandatory" (43).[3] A computer expert says rhetorically, "That Ryan guy is pretty smart, isn't he?" (492).

In addition to his brilliance, Ryan is always physically intrepid. He never hesitates to act, even in the most terrifying of situations. When the Capitol and government are destroyed, Ryan takes charge without a moment's pause. After sending his family to safety, he has himself sworn in as president and then gives a reassuring speech on television. He informs the world that America cannot be destroyed because of all the many parts that comprise her.

Other Americans

Typically, Clancy reintroduces characters in the FBI, in Congress and its staff, and the White House from earlier novels. Familiar military figures from out of the past join the action. Clancy brings people along as if they actually existed. They age, have children, retire, and some die. They are people from the army, navy, and air force. In *Without Remorse* a pilot and POW, Col. Robin Zacharias, was returned from Vietnam because of John Kelly/Clark. Now, a generation later, his son Mike is also a colonel and a pilot. Portagee Orteza, chief quartermaster in the Coast Guard in *Clear and Present Danger* as well as important player in *Without Remorse*, has retired. Living with his wife in Saipan, he once again is able to serve his country when the Japanese invade the island. Portagee, who knew John Kelly twenty years earlier and witnessed his "death," comes face-to-face with him once again.

American Spies

Spying remains an important part of the business of the CIA, which has agents in place in America, Russia, and Japan. Some of the spies are familiar, but there are also newcomers. One attractive young spy is Chet Nomuri, a fourth-generation Japanese American who speaks Japanese well enough to pass as a native. In his cover as a businessman, Nomuri spends a good bit of time gathering information in a Tokyo bathhouse frequented by people who know Prime Minister Goto. After learning about Goto's American mistress, Nomuri notifies others in the CIA network, who try in vain to save the young woman. It is also Nomuri who picks up vital information about Japanese attack plans against Russia. Further activities take him to outlying regions, where he photographs areas in which nuclear arms are stored. Through Nomuri's voice, the author compares life, customs, and attitudes in the United States and Japan. Not unexpectedly, Nomuri is grateful that his brave forebears selected the United States over Japan, even though they have not always been treated well in their country of choice.

Two CIA spies who have been sent to Japan are John Clark and Ding Chavez, both heroes from several other novels. Clark remains the leader, wiser, more skillful, and even more daring than his younger colleague. Chavez often finds Clark's knowledge awesome, even though Clark is an "old guy." For thirty years Clark has been a man in the field. None of his mental or physical effectiveness has flagged even though he might be trying to defy age by dying his hair. To those who have known him in the past, Clark remains something of an enigma. Beneath the veneer of civilization there is still "the hint of something else, like an animal in a cage, but an animal who knew how to pick the lock" (701). It was the bestial side of Clark that sought vengeance in his youth. His actions led to the necessity of "dying" and giving up his name *(Without Remorse).* After all these years, at Ryan's request, because of Clark's activities for his country, President Durling restores his real name—Kelly.

Now a middle-aged man with two grown daughters, Clark recognizes with regret that he must allow them to lead adult lives. His daughter Patricia Doris (Patsy)[4] wants to marry Ding Chavez, whom he likes and admires, but he isn't ready to part with his children. Still, when their mission is over, Clark tells Chavez he accepts reality, though reluctantly. After all, he recruited Chavez for the CIA, and the younger man has earned respect as well as admiration for his many achievements. Having come from the poor underclass, Chavez rose through the ranks in the army, joined the CIA, and became partner to Clark. Along the way he has even achieved a university education. In another of the many touches of local color, Clancy makes Chavez a graduate of George Mason University in Virginia.

The cover that both men have is that of Russian newsmen, a role Clark takes on like another skin. Additionally, when he makes contact with Japanese dissidents, he pretends to be a Russian intelligence office. As Russian newsman and agent, his name becomes Klerk, a variation of Clark. So convincing is he that even Chavez finds him a real Russian. Both men are self-sacrificing and extraordinary patriots, but Clark remains the superhero he was all those years ago in *Without Remorse*.

Traitors

The word "traitor" means different things depending on perspective. In Japan, the businessmen who manipulate elections in order to put in a puppet they control are not considered traitors by those they overthrow until they bring on a war. The foremost figure, Yamata, betrays everyone except his ancestors, whom he believes he is avenging. He destroys democratic government in Japan and ruins brokerage firms and banks. He almost decimates the world economy. Most important of all, it is through his maneuvers that world peace may collapse. Amoral and murderous, Yamata has no scruples about achieving his goal any way he can.

In contrast to Yamata's single-mindedness is the vacillation of treasonous Christopher Cook, an American deputy assistant secretary of state. No philosophical or historical reason drives his actions as they do Yamata's and those of some other Japanese. Cook leaks secret information through a Japanese diplomat because he wants more money than his job pays. He also expects more benefits later when he retires, expecting to emulate other influential Americans who have become lobbyists for foreign interests. Although he knows he has gone beyond acceptable diplomatic exchange of information, Cook rarely faces the reality of his betrayal. Consequences interest him only as they affect his life. Greed leads to his enmeshment step by step, and then fear of exposure keeps him in place.

STYLE

This eighth Clancy novel bears a greater resemblance to *Red Storm Rising* and *The Sum of All Fears* than to the immediately preceding novel *Without Remorse*. The scale is global, with several amorphous plots. Unnecessary details detract from the telling of the story. Do we need to know, for example, that Cathy Ryan's "laptop computer [is] an Apple Powerbook 800" (465)? Technical information abounds about the military, weapons—including missiles, manufacture of automobiles, and above all the stock market. Often the presentation of information appears to be in lecture format. One learns much of the workings of world banks and markets, useful and interesting facts for a textbook or course. However, here, as in other Clancy novels, the teaching technique slows down the action.

Language in the novel remains that of other Clancy works, from the familiar "old farts" to the now tiresome "shit happens." The authorial voice describes someone as a "technoweenie" (491), and a plane, cutely, as "the baddest helicopter" (84). Often terms sound repetitious, as with a favorite word—"pukes"—which appears frequently as a pejorative noun. For example, "I'm a State Department puke" (455). Clancy likes the description so much (or forgets he used it only a few lines earlier) that he has Ryan repeat it in his thoughts: "He was, after all, a State Department puke, and part of that culture" (456). There are also "intel puke[s]" (200), and "senior pukes" (561), and "yard puke[s]" (570). The language, though in vogue with the military, becomes tedious with repetition.

THEMES

The themes of *Debt of Honor* remind America of history as well as present and future danger. The victory of the Allies in World War II won't protect them now or later. A vigilant country is vital to its own preservation, we are told directly and indirectly throughout the novel. Episodes, dialogue, and commentary constantly drive the major theme: danger is all around. Attacks of all kinds can come from many areas and different countries, as is demonstrated in the novel not only through the actions of Japan but also by India. The United States is vulnerable militarily and economically.

The economic factor was central in the outbreak of World War II. Once again it is an issue in reality and in the novel. In trading, Japan has gained the upper hand over the United States. Instead of acting, we react, Clancy points out. Militarily the motion is less strong than in the past, and the theme reverberates with the warning that we are more vulnerable than we realize. Because of retrenchment in the last few years, the United States and its possessions may not be defensible against assaults, particularly if they occur on several fronts. Our military forces, built up for decades, now have been downsized. Ships, planes, and weapons have been scrapped. Nuclear agreements have not been monitored carefully enough, and while Russia is no longer a threat to us, her nuclear material is. Jack Ryan, the author's spokesman, sounds the warning bell to the president, and also to the reader, about the vulnerability of the United States under present circumstances. Even the thoughts of the monstrous Yamata reflect the theme: "Instead of merely maintaining their power, the Americans had cast it aside at the moment of its ascendancy, as they had so often in their history" (86).

ALTERNATE READING: FEMINIST CRITICISM

Feminists believe that women have been oppressed throughout the centuries. Most of the cultures of the world are patriarchal, with the male dominant, the female subordinate. Men have controlled women financially, intellectually, educationally, religiously, and physically. In the feminist view, men regard women as naturally inferior, products of biology, created as lesser beings. That concept of the natural order leads to the conclusion that gender is destiny, that women's lives are subject more to body than mind. (Some feminists extol the differences, seeing women as superior because they have life experiences unavailable to men, such as pregnancy and birth.)

For the past quarter of the century women have struggled to define their roles in all fields. In recent years feminist theories have been directed to examination and analysis of literature, of works written by both men and women. Feminist critics argue that literature reveals the ambivalence of writers toward the roles of women in society. Although men may speak of equality of the sexes in all aspects of life, often that is window dressing which masks actual personal and professional views and behavior. In multiple ways the writer may undercut what the story ostensibly tells the reader. Writers may announce that their audience consists of both males and females, yet the writer may address readers as if they were exclusively one sex or the other. That is evident in Clancy's fiction, in spite of the effort he makes to elevate the role of women.

Episodes, language, tone, and even commentary in fiction often reveal that two levels of thought are functioning simultaneously. Women may be shown as holding better jobs than men, yet they don't usually perform as well. Often, women are seen as less prepared, more emotional, less dedicated. Women may collapse under the strain of professional life. Not so for the man. No matter the talents of the woman the man is her central focus, whereas the same is not true for the man.

Under the name of feminist theory, Clancy's work can be explored in all these ways. If, as some critics suggest, there is a man's book and a woman's book, Clancy's is the former. He speaks to readers as if they were all male. In *Debt of Honor* as well as Clancy's other novels it is males who reflect significant aspects of American and Japanese society and their cultural attitudes. We see no Japanese women and hear little about them, as if they have no role in a masculine society.

A great gulf separates men and women in Japan. Using a tableaulike representation in a scene aboard a Japanese train, Clancy emphasizes that unreachable distance. On the train a man sits reading and openly enjoying pornographic material while a woman standing "right next to him" stares out a window. Neither exists for the other. The observer (Chet Nomuri) sees "the war between the sexes" in Japan as "different" from the gender war of the United States (101). In a book rife with information about a great many things, nothing further is said about relationships of Japanese men and women. Instead much is made of masculine interest in Western women, that is, in their bodies. Breasts are described whenever a scene in a bathhouse occurs. Little else about American women appears to interest Japanese men other than the size of their breasts. Breast size is not a new topic in a Clancy novel, but now he makes it a habitual, leering interest of the Japanese. In the bathhouse where Nomuri gathers information, conversation invariably centers on the erotic charms of the prime minister's American mistress. Although the reader is not privy to the stories told about the specific sexual behavior of the prime minister, enough hints are given to make it appear unusually lascivious. "I love fucking Americans," Goto says "coarsely"

(183). In *Debt of Honor* Japanese interest in Western culture gets reduced to bedding a young, blonde woman with "round eyes" (99).

Back in the United States, the author suggests that American women have powerful, important jobs, yet the text often undercuts that. In spite of the large number of women characters, their function in the novel is limited, with roles secondary to those of males. Clancy, not known for depth of treatment of any character, develops female characters even less than males. After giving something of a token nod to the placement of women in the American government, military, and news business he shows little interest in them.

Only Dr. Caroline Ryan, whom critic Christopher Buckley aptly labels "Ryan's saintly wife" (Oct. 2, 1994:28), is shown in any detail. She is the model wife, mother, physician, who also inspires her husband's most brilliant economic coup, which helps prevent world catastrophe. No other woman could possibly measure up to her. Is she realistic? Clearly not. She is a masculine fantasy of female perfection, who in her moment of greatest professional triumph compares the winning of the prestigious Lasker ophthalmology award to giving birth. Without stressing the point too much, one might consider this an extension, though unintentional, of the idea that biology is destiny. Jack Ryan saves the world, again and again in book after book, but he is never heard to compare his professional successes to fatherhood.

Mary Pat Foley, the deputy director for operations, CIA, and a fixture in Clancy's books, is less perfect than Cathy Ryan. Occasionally she makes mistakes, and on Sunday mornings she looks like any other woman—what is meant by this is unclear. Should the tone be heard as unfriendly, or does the author believe he is praising her by suggesting she is the image of other females except for her impressive position? When Clancy remarks that Mrs. Foley has the senior job and her husband the lesser one, she is described as having better instincts and he as being better at planning (69). In other words, the male is superior in logic and reasoning, a patriarchal view that permeates literature, culture, education, psychology, and politics. Clancy knows well that feminists will seize on such comments about female intuition, for he has a scene in which Ryan and a female reporter discuss it. When the reporter says she believes some of the sexual rumors surrounding the Japanese prime minister, Ryan jokes about female intuition. The reporter, annoyed, accuses him of being sexist. Ryan's response is to deny that, because after all his wife is better at judging people than he is (221). Clancy wants to have it both ways, to feel free to use the old canard about women and then to protect himself against being called antifeminist.

In his comparison of the two Foleys, Clancy follows up the statement on instinct by remarking that the jobs should have been reversed, with the husband as senior, but politics entered into the appointment of the wife. In other words, the choice of Mary Pat was one of political correctness. Clancy seems to have forgotten that Mrs. Foley has earned her position through the hard work and achievements of her early career. What is more, he as her creator has made her what she is, an intelligent, imaginative, skilled agent who rose through the ranks to power. But even as her literary "father" he cannot forgo the patriarchal attitude.

Political correctness has been ascribed to the author for his inclusion of large numbers of women in the novel. In addition to Cathy Ryan and Mary Pat Foley there are female staff assistants, secretaries, FBI agents, reporters, a psychologist, and an air force major who jokes like a man. Clancy can't resist having his own little joke in the naming of a female officer, Navy Commander Peach. Although he might see himself as a defender of American womanhood, when he returns at several points to crimes against women, the reader wonders about the psychological attraction/repulsion factors in these activities. The two side-by-side subplots in America and Japan, involving drugs, rape, coercion, suicide, and even murder in part may have some factual, documented basis. All the moral males in the novel find these deeds abhorrent and voice concern about the ugliness of such acts. Yet, there is little follow-up on their indignation. As a result the impact of the presentation, the language, the episodes and their resolution is familiarly oppressive, as they invoke old attitudes and injustices toward women.

Powerful men use and abuse American women, both in the United States and Japan. It doesn't matter that the women at home are older, wealthier professionals and the one in Japan is a teenager, a runaway in search of excitement. The women appear similar in their helplessness as seemingly invincible men in each country destroy their lives. Although feminist critics generally regard descriptions of sexual violence against women as pornography, Clancy's novel does not depict the minutia of torture or rape. He leaves it to the reader to fill in the gaps as he uses the word "rape" again and again in detailing the scenes at home and abroad. However, more specificity and suggestiveness appear in the sexual events that occur in Japan. The young woman's body is seen close up alive and in even greater detail after her murder. A word here, a phrase there—the fluid on her thighs, her robe open on her nudity—

tells of her degradation. All of this supports the suggestion that the Japanese are more brutal than Americans are to women. We are told they enjoy reading about "kinky" sex. People comment on the prime minister's weird sexual tastes. In such an atmosphere it is not surprising that vicious Japanese criminals casually gang-rape an American woman before murdering her.

In the larger picture of war that fills the novel, of course the decimated lives of a few females are unimportant. Still it is disquieting that the perpetrators suffer little or not at all. Vengeance is taken against them in *Without Remorse*, but these rapists escape, if not scot-free, then almost so. Clancy was criticized for the brutal morality in that earlier book in which rapists who seduced, drugged, and murdered women met stern justice. *Debt of Honor* goes in a different direction. Here, it is the women who pay, and pay, and pay.

NOTES

1. In reality, Japan has invested heavily in the United States, as Clancy shows in the novel. Some of the investments have been unsuccessful. Others, although good revenue producers, have been unsuitable to the temperament of the Japanese businesspeople. Investment in the movie industry, MCA, for example is a case in point. Japanese businesspeople could not adapt to Hollywood business practices.

2. People who have watched Clancy interviews on television will recognize him in the portrait of Ryan (684), in whom he has said he sees himself.

3. Yalies appear to aggravate the author. He singles them out in other books also.

4. The double name should be suggestive to someone who has read *Without Remorse*. Clark's first wife was called Trish, an affectionate nickname for Patricia. And Doris was the name of a young woman Clark tried to rescue from drug dealers. Ironically, in that novel, he doesn't seem to like the name. Perhaps the author is having his little joke, as he often does with names.

Bibliography

WORKS BY TOM CLANCY

Clancy, Tom. *Armored Cav*. New York: Berkley Books, 1994.

———. "Back to the Frontier." *The Tom Clancy Companion*, 113–115. Ed. Martin H. Greenberg. New York: Berkley Books, 1992.

———. "Before Anyone Gets Carried Away." *The Tom Clancy Companion*, 87–91. Ed. Martin H. Greenberg. New York: Berkley Books, 1992.

———. "But I *Like* to Shoot." *The Tom Clancy Companion*, 116–120. Ed. Martin H. Greenberg. New York: Berkley Books, 1992.

———. *The Cardinal of the Kremlin*. New York: G. P. Putnam's Sons, 1988.

———. *The Cardinal of the Kremlin* (excerpt). *Popular Mechanics*, Aug. 1988: 93–100.

———. *Clear and Present Danger*. New York: G. P. Putnam's Sons, 1989.

———. *Debt of Honor*. New York: G. P. Putnam's Sons, 1994.

———. "Dinosaurs." *The Tom Clancy Companion*, 144–147. Ed. Martin H. Greenberg. New York: Berkley Books, 1992.

———. "The Federal News Service." *The Tom Clancy Companion*, 121–128. Ed. Martin H. Greenberg. New York: Berkley Books, 1992.

———. *Fighter Wing*. New York: Berkley Books, 1995.

———. "Funerals." *The Tom Clancy Companion*, 140–143. Ed. Martin H. Greenberg. New York: Berkley Books, 1992.

———. "Getting Our Money's Worth." *The Tom Clancy Companion*, 107–112. Ed. Martin H. Greenberg. New York: Berkley Books, 1992.

————. *The Hunt for Red October*. Annapolis: Naval Institute Press, 1984.

————. "Isvestia—1." *The Tom Clancy Companion*, 129–131. Ed. Martin H. Greenberg. New York: Berkley Books, 1992.

————. "Isvestia—2. Capitalism: The Economics Olympics." *The Tom Clancy Companion*, 132–135. Ed. Martin H. Greenberg. New York: Berkley Books, 1992.

————. "Isvestia—3. Principles." *The Tom Clancy Companion*, 136–139. Ed. Martin H. Greenberg. New York: Berkley Books, 1992.

————. *Patriot Games*. New York: G. P. Putnam's Sons, 1987.

————. *Patriot Games* (excerpt). *Good Housekeeping*, Feb. 1988: 163–166+.

————. *Reality Check: What's Going On Out There?* New York: Putnam Publishing Group, 1995.

————. *Red Storm Rising*. New York: G. P. Putnam's Sons, 1986.

————. *Submarine*. New York: Berkley Books, 1993.

————. *The Sum of All Fears*. New York: G. P. Putnam's Books, 1991.

————. *Tom Clancy's Op Center*. Created by Tom Clancy and Steve Pieczenik. New York: Berkley Books, 1995.

————. *Tom Clancy's Op Center: Mirror Image*. Created by Tom Clancy and Steve Pieczenik. New York: Berkley Books, 1995.

————. "Turn Back." *The Tom Clancy Companion*, 148–155. Ed. Martin H. Greenberg. New York: Berkley Books, 1992.

————. *Without Remorse*. New York: G. P. Putnam's Sons, 1993.

————, and Russell Seitz. "Five Minutes Past Midnight—and Welcome to the Age of Proliferation." *The Tom Clancy Companion*, 92–106. Ed. Martin H. Greenberg. New York: Berkley Books, 1992.

WORKS ABOUT TOM CLANCY

Alson, Peter, and Christopher Phillips. "As His Latest Flight of Fancy Goes on Sale, Tom Clancy Eyes a Job in Space." *People Weekly*, 28 Aug. 1989: 86–88.

Bennett, Ralph Kinney. "Tom Clancy's Dream Come True." *Reader's Digest*, Feb. 1989: 126–131.

Bond, Larry. "Introduction." *The Tom Clancy Companion*, 1–4. Ed. Martin H. Greenberg. New York: Berkley Books, 1992.

Carlson, Peter. "What Ticks Tom Clancy Off?" *Washington Post Magazine*, 27 June 1993: 12+.

Cooper, Marc. "Interview: Tom Clancy." *Playboy*, April 1988: 55–57+.

Cox, Meg. "The Real Bad Guys Work in Hollywood." *Wall Street Journal*, 22 Jan. 1992: A1+.

Ferrell, Keith. "Conversations: Going to War with Tom Clancy." *Compute*, Nov. 1988: 14–15.

Friend, Tad. "The Pentagon's Favorite Novelist." *Gentlemen's Quarterly* 58.6 (June 1988): 220–223+.

Greenberg, Martin. "An Interview with Tom Clancy." *The Tom Clancy Companion*, 57–86. Ed. Martin H. Greenberg. New York: Berkley Books, 1992.

Interview. *Good Morning America*. ABC. 21 April 1995.

Interview. *This Morning*. CBS. 18 Aug. 1994.

Interviews. *Larry King Live*. CNN. 16 Aug. 1993; 18 Aug. 1994; 24 Feb. 1995.

Kornheiser, Tony. "Girls and Guise." *Washington Post*, 9 Oct. 1994: F1.

Levine, Art. "The Pentagon's Unlikely Hero." *U.S. News and World Report*, 15 Sept. 1986: 66.

"The Literary Life: How the Other Half Writes." *Esquire*, July 1989: 82–89.

Mansfield, Stephanie. "Fax Fire." *Washington Post*, 6 Oct. 1994: B1+.

———. "He's Been There, Done That." *Washington Post*, 27 Feb. 1995: B1–2.

Mattox, William R., Jr. "Family vs. Work: Don't Leave Dads Out of the Picture." *Wall Street Journal*, 12 June 1991: A14.

Max, Daniel. "Is Clancy Chancy at $14 Million?" *Variety*, 3 Aug. 1992: 1+.

Mutter, John. "PW Interviews Tom Clancy." *Publishers Weekly*, 8 Aug. 1986: 53–54.

Rogers, Patricia Dane. "Tom Clancy's Cliffhanger of a House." *Washington Post*, 4 Oct. 1990: 20+.

Ryan, William. "The Genesis of the Techno-Thriller." *Virginia Quarterly Review* 69.1 (Winter 1993): 24–40.

Shales, Tom. "Eeny-Meeny: A Mini Showdown." *Washington Post*, 26 Feb. 1995: G1+.

Shuger, Scott. "Paperback Fighter." *Washington Monthly*, Nov. 1989: 10–18.

Thomas, Evan. "The Art of the Techno-Thriller." *Newsweek*, 8 Aug. 1988: 60–65.

Thomas, Karen. "Clancy Clams Up On-Line." *USA Today*, 20 April 1995: 2D.

———. "Clancy Marriage in Present Danger." *USA Today*, 19 April 1995: 2D.

Ward, Cynthia. "Author Tom Clancy and His Novels in Defense of America." *Conservative Digest*, April 1988: 5–12.

Wile, Mary Lee Hanford. "A Proud Parent Laments: Where Was George?" *Education Week*, 12 Sept. 1990: 27+.

"The Write Stuff." Interview. *American Legion*, Dec. 1991: 16–17+.

REVIEWS AND CRITICISM

General

Anderson, Patrick. "King of the Techno-Thriller." *New York Times Magazine*, 1 May 1988: 54+.

Cerasini, Marc. "Tom Clancy's Fiction." *The Tom Clancy Companion*, 5–55. Ed. Martin H. Greenberg. New York: Berkley Books, 1992.

Cook, William J., and Robert Kaylor. "How to Stop a Russian 'Surge.' " *U.S. News and World Report*, 15 June 1987: 43.

Donnelly, Joe. "A Night for a Little Intrigue." *Washington Post,* 27 July 1994: D1–2.

Hixson, Walter. *"Red Storm Rising:* Tom Clancy Novels and the Cult of National Security." *Diplomatic History* 17.4 (Fall 1993): 599–613.

Ross, Jean. "Tom Clancy." *Contemporary Authors,* vol. 131, 109–113. Detroit: Gale Research, 1991.

Sandza, Richard. "Does the Word Warrior Get His Facts Right?" *Newsweek,* 8 Aug. 1988: 62–63.

The Cardinal of the Kremlin

Books. Review of *The Cardinal of the Kremlin. Playboy,* Sept. 1988: 21.

Ferguson, Andrew. "Tom Clancy's Star Wars Story." Review of *The Cardinal of the Kremlin. Fortune,* 18 July 1988: 101–102.

Graves, James. Review of *The Cardinal of the Kremlin. Conservative Digest,* May 1989: 65.

Novak, Ralph. "Picks and Pans." Review of *The Cardinal of the Kremlin. People Weekly,* 12 Sept. 1988: 35–39.

Skow, John. "Son of Megatech." *Time,* 25 July 1988: EB3.

Clear and Present Danger

Carcaterra, Lorenza. Review of *Clear and Present Danger. People Weekly,* 16 Oct. 1989: 31–32.

Hagman, Harvey. "Tom Clancy Declares War on Colombian Drug Trade." Review of *Clear and Present Danger. Washington Times,* 23 Aug. 1989: E1–2.

Lee, James Ward. "Techno-Thriller Explores the Colombian War on Drugs." Review of *Clear and Present Danger. Houston Post,* 10 Sept. 1989: C6.

Maslin, Janet. "Ryan Spies Again, This Time as C.I.A. Battles Drug Lords." Review of film *Clear and Present Danger. New York Times,* 3 Aug. 1994: C11+.

Shapiro, Walter. "Of Arms and the Man." Review of *Clear and Present Danger. Time,* 21 Aug. 1989: 66–68.

Shulman, Randy. *"Clear and Present Danger:* The Obvious Winner." Review of film *Clear and Present Danger. Times Community Newspapers Weekender,* 10 Aug. 1994: 11.

Thomas, Evan. "Dealing with the Druggies." Review of *Clear and Present Danger. Newsweek,* 21 Aug. 1989: 60.

Thomas, Ross. Review of *Clear and Present Danger. Washington Post Book World,* 13 Aug. 1989: 1.

Williams, Dick. "Tom Clancy's New Novel Offers Real War on Drugs." Review of *Clear and Present Danger*. *Atlanta Journal and Constitution*, 14 Dec. 1989: A23.

Wise, David. "Just Say Nuke 'Em." Review of *Clear and Present Danger*. *New York Times Book Review*, 13 Aug. 1989: 9.

Debt of Honor

Buckley, Christopher. "Megabashing Japan." Review of *Debt of Honor*. *New York Times Book Review*, 2 Oct. 1994: 7:28.

Helmick, Kristiana. "Running Out of Foes, Clancy Picks on Japan." Review of *Debt of Honor*. *Christian Science Monitor*, 2 Aug. 1994: 15.

Jones, Steve. "Economic Warfare Escalates in Clancy's 'Debt.' " Review of *Debt of Honor*. *USA Today*, 18 Aug. 1994: D1.

Kaplan, Howard. "In a Word, Clancy Still Long-Winded." Review of *Debt of Honor*. *Denver Post*, 21 Aug. 1994: E10.

Lee, James Ward. "*Debt of Honor* an Exercise in Classic Clancy." Review of *Debt of Honor*. *Houston Post*, 18 Sept. 1994: C5.

Shelton, Judy. "A Run for the Money." Review of *Debt of Honor*. *Washington Post Book World*, 1 Oct. 1994: H1–2.

The Hunt for Red October

Adelman, Ken. "Real Enough to Be Classified." Review of *The Hunt for Red October*. *Washington Times*, 12 March 1990: 1.

Alden, John. "The Cold War at 50 Fathoms." Review of *The Hunt for Red October*. *Wall Street Journal*, 22 Oct. 1984: 28.

Hinson, Hal. "*Red October*: Full Speed Ahead." Review of film *The Hunt for Red October*. *Washington Post*, 2 March 1990: D1.

Setlowe, Richard. Review of *The Hunt for Red October*. *Los Angeles Times Book Review*, 9 Dec. 1984: 2.

Sherman, John. Review of *The Hunt for Red October*. *West Coast Review of Books* 10.16 (November-December 1984): 30.

Wainwright, Loudon. "A Fantasy Fit for a President." Review of *The Hunt for Red October*. *Life*, April 1985: 7+.

Patriot Games

Lehman, David. "Taking On the Terrorists." Review of *Patriot Games*. *Newsweek*, 17 Aug. 1987: 68.

McCarthy, John. Books in Brief. Review of *Patriot Games*. *National Review*, 29 April 1989: 53.

Steinberg, Sybil. Forecasts. Review of *Patriot Games*. *Publishers Weekly*, 5 June 1987: 71.

Thomas, Ross. "White Knight, Green Villains." Review of *Patriot Games*. *New York Times Book Review*, 2 Aug. 1987: 11.

Red Storm Rising

Arias, Ron. "Afloat in *Red October*'s Wake, Tom Clancy Skippers His Second Thriller Right to the Top." Review of *Red Storm Rising*. *People Weekly*, 8 Sept. 1986: 85–87.

Glassman, James. "Tom Clancy Gets Fancy." Review of *Red Storm Rising*. *USA Today*, 18 July 1986: 4D.

Isaacson, Walter. "When the Shooting Stops." Review of *Red Storm Rising*. *Time*, 11 Aug. 1986: 64.

Keegan, John. "Tom Clancy Hunts Again." Review of *Red Storm Rising*. *Washington Post Book World*, 27 July 1986: 1–2.

Lehman, David. "Plotting the Ultimate War Game." Review of *Red Storm Rising*. *Newsweek*, 25 Aug. 1986: 64.

Lehman-Haupt, Christopher. Books of the Times. Review of *Red Storm Rising*. *New York Times Book Review*, 17 July 1986: C21.

Lekachman, Robert. "Virtuous Men and Perfect Weapons." Review of *Red Storm Rising*. *New York Times Book Review*, 27 July 1986: 7–8.

Williams, Andrew. "T. E. Lawrence and Tom Clancy." *T. E. Notes: A T. E. Lawrence Newsletter* 3.1 (1992): 3.

The Sum of All Fears

Kaplan, Howard. "Clancy's Newest Book May Be His Best." Review of *The Sum of All Fears*. *Denver Post*, 11 Aug. 1991: 2.

Lee, James Ward. "Tom Clancy's Thrillers Keep Getting Better." Review of *The Sum of All Fears*. *Houston Post*, 15 Sept. 1991: C5.

Meeks, Fleming. "Golden Prose." Review of *The Sum of All Fears*. *Forbes*, 19 Aug. 1991: 42.

Menand, Louis. "Very Popular Mechanics." Review of *The Sum of All Fears*. *The New Yorker*, 16 Sept. 1991: 91–95.

O'Brian, Patrick. "Once More on the Brink." Review of *The Sum of All Fears*. *Washington Post Book World*, 28 July 1991: X1.

Williamson, Ted. "Long Fuse to Doomsday." Review of *The Sum of All Fears*. *Detroit News and Free Press*, 28 July 1991: Q7.

Without Remorse

Arana-Ward, Marie. "Tom Clancy's Avenging Angel." Review of *Without Remorse*. *Washington Post Book World*, 8 Aug. 1993: X1.

Ellis, Bob. "Clancy Develops a Shadowy Figure and Taut Action." Review of *Without Remorse*. *Detroit News and Free Press*, 8 Aug. 1993: H7.

Hilbert, Daniel. "*Without Remorse:* Tom Clancy Aims to Kill." Review of *Without Remorse*. *Detroit News and Free Press*, 11 Aug. 1993: C3.

Liddy, Gordon. "The Smell of Napalm in the Morning." Review of *Without Remorse*. *New York Times Book Review*, 22 Aug. 1993: 13.

Schwartz, Gil. "What to Read on the Beach: Clancy vs. Le Carré." Review of *Without Remorse*. *Fortune*, 9 Aug. 1993: 98.

Steinberg, Sybil. Forecasts. Review of *Without Remorse*. *Publishers Weekly*, 28 June 1993: 59.

OTHER SECONDARY SOURCES

Aisenberg, Nadya. *A Common Spring: Crime Novel and Classic*. Bowling Green, Ohio: Bowling Green University Popular Press, 1979.

Amis, Kingsley. *The James Bond Dossier*. New York: New American Library, 1965.

Brantinger, Patrick. *Bread and Circuses*. 3rd printing. Ithaca, New York: Cornell University Press, 1993.

Brinkley, Alan. "The View from the Former Top." Review of *Special Trust* by Robert McFarlane. *New York Times Book Review*, 13 Nov. 1994: 9.

Buckley, Christopher. "The Con Channel." *The New Yorker*, 12 Dec. 1994: 136.

———. From "If Your Life Were a Book," *Washington Post Book World*, 4 Dec. 1994: 1+.

Collier, Peter, and Helga Geyer-Ryan, eds. *Literary Theory Today*. Ithaca, New York: Cornell University Press, 1990.

Dickstein, Morris. *Double Agent: The Critic and Society*. New York: Oxford University Press, 1992.

Eagleton, Terry. *Literary Theory*. Minneapolis: University of Minnesota Press, 1983.

Ellman, Mary. *Thinking about Women*. New York: Harcourt Brace Jovanovich, 1968.

Felman, Shoshana, ed. *Literature and Psychoanalysis*. Baltimore: Johns Hopkins University Press, 1982.

Fleming, Ian. *Casino Royale*. New York: Charter Books, 1987.

Freud, Sigmund. *Five Lectures on Psycho-Analysis*. New York: W. W. Norton, n.d.

————. *The Freud Reader*. Ed. Peter Gay. New York: W. W. Norton, 1989.

————. *Inhibitions, Symptoms and Anxiety*. New York: W. W. Norton, 1959.

Gallop, Jane. *The Daughter's Seduction: Feminism and Psychoanalysis*. Ithaca, New York: Cornell University Press, 1992.

Graham, Bradley. "Republicans Plot Military Maneuvers." *Washington Post*, 12 Dec. 1994: A21.

Harper, Ralph. *The World of the Thriller*. Baltimore: Johns Hopkins University Press, 1979.

Himmelfarb, Gertrude. *The New History and the Old*. Cambridge, Mass.: Harvard University Press, 1987.

Jung, Carl G. *Man and His Symbols*. New York: Dell, 1971.

Lacan, Jacques. *The Four Fundamental Concepts of Psycho-Analysis*. W. W. Norton, 1981.

McFarlane, Robert, and Zofia Smardz. *Special Trust*. New York: Cadell and Davies, 1994.

Panek, LeRoy. *The Special Branch*. Bowling Green, Ohio: Bowling Green University Popular Press, 1981.

Reeves, Charles Eric. "Myth Theory and Criticism." *The Johns Hopkins Guide to Literary Theory and Criticism*, 520–523. Ed. Michael Groden and Martin Kreisworth. Baltimore: Johns Hopkins University Press, 1994.

Rupprecht, Carol Schreir. "Archetypal Theory and Criticism." *The Johns Hopkins Guide to Literary Theory and Criticism*, 36–40. Ed. Michael Groden and Martin Kreisworth. Baltimore: Johns Hopkins University Press, 1994.

Shultz, George P. *Turmoil and Triumph*. New York: Charles Scribner's Sons, 1993.

Skura, Meredith Anne. *The Literary Use of the Psychoanalytic Process*. New Haven: Yale University Press, 1981.

Suleiman, Susan, and Inge Crosman, eds. *The Reader in the Text*. Princeton: Princeton University Press, 1980.

Suvin, Darko. *Metamorphosis of Science Fiction*. New Haven and London: Yale University Press, 1979.

Symons, Julian. *Mortal Consequences*. New York: Schocken Books, 1973.

Todorov, Tzvetan. *The Fantastic: A Structural Approach to a Literary Genre*. Cleveland: Case Western Reserve University Press, 1973.

Index

ABOUT THE AUTHOR

HELEN S. GARSON is Professor Emeritus of English and American Studies at George Mason University in Fairfax, Virginia. She is author of *The Short Fiction of Truman Capote* (1992), *Truman Capote* (1981), and numerous articles about Truman Capote. She has written about John Le Carré, John Hawkes, Flannery O'Connor, gothic, spy, and detective novels, pornography, popular culture, and American women novelists.